Home
Woodworking

Home Woodworking

Fred Sherlock

Newnes Technical Books

Newnes Technical Books

is an imprint of the Butterworth Group

which has principal offices in

London, Sydney, Toronto, Wellington, Durban and Boston

First published 1982

British Library Cataloguing in Publication Data

Sherlock, Fred
    Home woodworking.
    1. Woodwork – Amateurs' manuals
    I. Title
    684'.08   TT185

ISBN 0-408-01121-1

Typeset by Butterworths Litho Preparation Department
Printed in England by Redwood Burn Ltd., Trowbridge

Preface

They say that home is what you make it, and for most of us this involves a considerable amount of work. Professional services are expensive, and from this stems the great incentive to tackle as much as possible yourself. If you can reduce costs to materials and tools only, this will have two immediate effects.

First, you will have money available for other projects. Second, you may have more money with which to buy better-quality materials – and add to your tool kit.

The term do-it-yourself encompasses a very wide range of activities, and there is much to learn. It is not always easy, but once new skills have been mastered, work becomes both rewarding and satisfying.

All the books in this series have been written by people with very considerable practical experience, and many of the authors have been involved in feature writing for the magazine *Do it yourself*, now past its 25th birthday. They have also been responsible for answering hundreds of reader's enquiries, which has given them an insight into the real needs and problems encountered in and about the house.

I'm sure you will find their advice invaluable. May I wish you success in all you undertake.

Tony Wilkins
Editor, 'Do it yourself' magazine

Contents

Introduction   1

Basic tool list   2

1   Basic tools: hand and electric   3

2   Choosing materials   13

3   Fittings and fixings   22

4   Jointing solid wood and chipboard   30

5   Using tools for joint-cutting   41

6   Assembly methods   51

7   Working drawings and marking out   60

8   Surface finishing   71

9   Practical projects   79

Index   97

Introduction

There are many books aimed towards helping the novice home woodworker to learn of the tools and of the processes involved. Some are aimed at the person who wants to become a specialist – a cabinet maker, a carpenter or a joiner. There are also books for wood turners and books for the wood polisher.

Each of these has its special approach. The approach of this book is to help those who feel the need to improve their homes by their own efforts and who are inclined to learn just sufficient to enable them to make a reasonable success of such projects as they undertake.

If, in the event, the reader who starts out as one of these not-too-enthusiastic woodworkers becomes enthralled (as he must, for woodworking is addictive), then the step-by-step approach of the book will lead him carefully on.

The projects that conclude the book start with one that is fully documented and end with one that is suggested only in outline, for these projects are intended only for learning practice. Once started, there will be no end.

Good luck!

Basic tool list

'Workmate' bench or solid workshop bench
Steel tape, 2 m (Imperial and metric)
Steel rule, 1 m (Imperial and metric)
Handsaw, 560 mm (22 in), 7–8 points
Tenon (back) saw, 300 mm (12 in)
Steel jack plane No 5½, 60 mm (2⅜ in) iron
Steel smoothing plane No 4, 60 mm (2⅜ in) iron
Steel try square, 150 mm (6 in) with 45° mitre shoulder
Spirit level
Plumb bob and line
Mortise gauge, twin spur and single spur
Marking knife
Sliding bevel
Cabinet screwdriver, 150 mm (6 in)
Small screwdriver, 100 mm (4 in)
Pozidriv/Supadriv screwdriver
Bench hook, self-made
Mortise chisels, 6, 9 and 12 mm (¼, ⅜ and ½ in)
Mallet
Bevel edge chisels, 6, 12 and 25 mm (¼, ½ and 1 in), wood/plastic handles
Firmer chisels, 9 and 18 mm (⅜ and ¾ in), wood/plastic handles
Cork sanding block
Twist drills, 3, 4.5, 6, 7.5 and 9 mm (⅛, 3⁄16, ¼, 5⁄16 and ⅜ in)

Jennings bits, 9, 12, 18, 25 and 32 mm (⅜, ½, ¾, 1 and 1¼ in)
Hand drill (wheel brace)
Hand brace, 250 mm (10 in) swing
Screwdriver bits
Warrington hammer
Mitre box, self-made
Shooting board, self-made
Pincers
Cabinet scraper
Nail set and punch
Bradawl
Coping saw
Block-sharpening stone, medium.
The three wooden aids – the mitre box, the shooting board and the bench hook – should be given two or three coats of raw linseed oil. This builds up surface protection, improves their appearance and helps to keep them clean.

Later additions

Two-speed hammer or variable-speed drill
Tungsten carbide masonry drills
Circular saw attachment
Sander attachment
Jigsaw attachment
Grinding attachment
Vertical drill stand
Drill base to take drill in horizontal position
(Special purpose tools are far superior to a drill with attachments. But before buying always consider the extent to which the equipment will be used.)

Chapter 1
Basic tools: hand and electric

Tools for all trades are acquired gradually. Some are bought, some are given, some are inherited, some are made and some are even swapped as experience shows those that will be needed most and those that are not needed at all. In this chapter the basic tool requirements are made clear and the use of the main tools is described. Simple instructions are introduced to given examples of tool usage.

General tools

Before any job of woodworking can be tackled a workbench is essential. The old kitchen table was once the standard equipment but today there are no such things – drop-leaf chipboard, faced with resin laminate, is useless. A bench is a must.

Unless garage space is available where a substantial, heavyweight, solid wooden bench may be made and installed, there is no better item than the Black and Decker 'Workmate'. For years I resisted the well-meant advice to buy one, a standard bench being already available and in use. But suddenly one was offered, and since that day the 'Workmate' has rarely been folded unless for travelling; it has earned its place over and over again (and this is

the sincere and objective view of a life-long woodworker).

Storage

Storage of tools is best in racks, if space is available. If not, store in the traditional carpenter's box, but protect saw teeth with grooved plastic strips and chisel edges with plastic chisel guards.

Saws

Saws cut their way through wood using their teeth. As long as the teeth are right for the job – and sharp – the job is easily and accurately performed. The wood grain along a board is long grain; across the board it is short, or cross, grain. Each run of the grain requires a different tooth shape. Long grain needs to be chiselled away chip by chip, whereas cross grain falls easily away once both ends of a short fibre are severed. Thus saw teeth for rip-sawing (long-grain sawing) need to

Folding workbench, with tenon cheeks being sawn with a panel saw

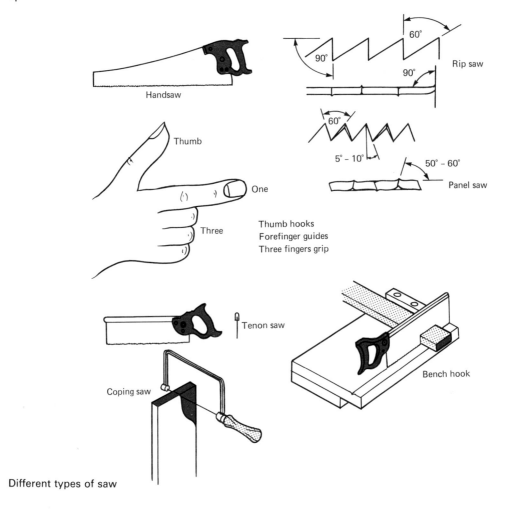

Handsaw

Thumb

One

Three

Thumb hooks
Forefinger guides
Three fingers grip

60°

90°

90°

Rip saw

60°

5° – 10°

50° – 60°

Panel saw

Tenon saw

Coping saw

Bench hook

Different types of saw

have almost square-topped chisel teeth and saw teeth for cross-cutting need to have needle points.

The tooth size – points per 25 mm (1 in) – will control the speed of cut and the quality of the sawn finish. Large teeth cut roughly but fast; small teeth cut smoothly, but slow.

Sawing jobs

Every piece of wood needs cutting to length and width and saws are made for this job; they are called handsaws. They have no back strip and keep stiff by inner tension rolled in during manufacture. They are tapered for balance in the hand.

A useful hint at this stage is to learn and use the old craftsman rule – thumb, one, three. The thumb hooks, the forefinger guides the three other fingers grip. This is the standard grip for many tools.

The saw lengths may be stamped on the blade close to the handle, together with a number that gives the number of tooth points to every 25 mm (1 in). The best general buy is a 560 mm (22 in) saw with seven or eight teeth to every 25 mm (1 in). Remember that large teeth are more easily sharpened than small teeth. The saw suggested, which has cross-cutting teeth, is suitable for most home carpentry. Note the tooth shape shown in the diagram; saws with finer teeth are called panel saws.

Back saws have parallel blades with stiffening back strips. These back strips are traditionally of brass, but for economy are now of mild steel. The blade depth is related to blade length – the longer, the deeper. Teeth are reasonably standard, with angles designed for cross-cutting rather than rip-sawing. Teeth are small and the larger saws have fewer points than smaller one. Choose a deep saw for first choice, one about 300 mm (12 in) long, which will have 10–12 points. Later a smaller saw with finer teeth will be useful. These back saws are commonly known as tenon saws for the larger sizes and dovetail saws for the smaller sizes.

For shaping cuts get a coping saw. This has a steel bow, which acts as a spring to keep the fine blade taut, and a turned wooden handle for holding. The blade clips into the frame. The teeth of this saw should point towards the handle and the cutting stroke is made by pulling the saw. The coping saw will attack most shapes willingly, but finesse in handling must be learned quickly, for blades break easily.

To save use of the precision saws, the jobbing DIY folding saw is useful, for it cuts both rough wood and the softer metals. It has a blade that folds back inside the handle when not in use.

Planes

Planes get their name from their purpose, which is to produce flat planes (geometrically flat surfaces). There are planes for taking rough wood down to size leaving all faces smooth. After joints are cut and the job is assembled, total surfaces are smoothed again, this time with a smaller plane. If long edges must be planed straight, very long planes are an advantage. Other plane types are for shaping wood to section or to shape, and there are yet others for fine-cutting into corners or for other intricate work.

How a plane works

Planes achieve their purpose because their soles are flat. A flat surface moved along in a straight line will, if it has a projecting cutting edge, produce a flat and straight surface. Like all tools, however, the results given by the plane depend on the skill of its use.

The sole is flat. The cutter, called the plane iron, projects slightly through a slot in the sole. As the plane is pushed forward the iron splits a fine shaving from the wood. This shaving is fed up through the plane and ejected. However, wood being wood, the angle of grain varies and the shaving splits to varying thicknesses. If this splitting extends below the nominal shaving thickness, it tears rather than is cut, and leaves a bad surface. To prevent this the slot in the plane sole is just wide enough for the iron to project and the chip to egress. This limits maximum chip thickness.

In addition to this iron, the plane has a back-iron. This is another plate (similar to the iron) which is bolted to the iron and set so that its extreme lower edge rests about 0.5 mm back from the cutting iron edge. The emergent shaving makes contact with this back-iron edge and is turned back on itself drastically (hence the rolled-up shaving). Because of this, the shaving now has insufficient strength to split, or tear out, below the nominal planing line and the surface remains smooth.

This principle is true for most planes.

Plane types

The first planing and sizing of wood is done with the jack plane. Several sizes of this are available and sizes are given numbers by all plane makers. The popular size for home work is No 5½, which is a plane 380 mm (15 in) long, with an iron width of 60 mm (2⅜ in). Finest smoothing and levelling of surfaces, after assembly and before sanding, is done by the smoothing plane, a smaller size than the jack. A common size is the No 4, which has a length of 260 mm (10½ in) and an iron width of 60 mm (2⅜ in). For fine cabinet work, the No 3 is better, being not so heavy. This has a length of 240 mm (9½

Planes, try square, mortise gauge and sliding bevel

in) and an iron width of 45 mm (1¾ in). These two planes should cover most jobbing carpentry.

Special planes

The long jointer or try plane (No 7) is for making long straight edges. Its length is 560 mm (22 in) and its iron width is 60 mm (2⅜ in). The special-purpose planes are the shoulder plane, the plough plane, the compass plane, the block plane, the bullnose plane, the rebating (fillister) plane, the side-rebate plane and the combination plane, which combines the rebate, plough and moulding planes.

The rebating plane rebates along edges of boards. The plough plane grooves along

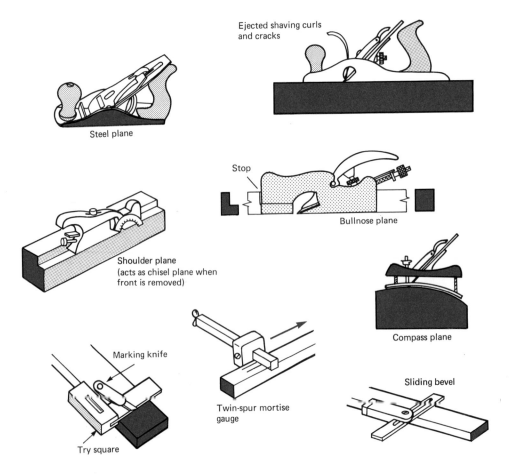

Steel plane

Ejected shaving curls and cracks

Shoulder plane (acts as chisel plane when front is removed)

Stop

Bullnose plane

Compass plane

Marking knife

Try square

Twin-spur mortise gauge

Sliding bevel

boards. The compass plane has an adjustable sole to suit varying curve radii. The block plane is a low-angle (of its iron) plane for single-handed use on any of the little bits of wood that need removing. The shoulder plane planes into shoulders and will deepen rebates. The bullnose plane will plane up to its cutting edge into snug joints and odd corners. The side-rebate will plane the sides of rebates without planing the bottom. The combination plane will do rebating, grooving and moulding. All these may be added to the kit as it is found necessary.

To avoid the job of sharpening plane blades it is possible to buy a plane that uses disposable blades, each of which is used until blunt. These can be replaced at low cost.

Marking tools

These tools explain themselves. Rules – steel ones are best – are used for measuring. Tapes are useful for long line measurement but are not easily used for marking. The try square is most useful if it has a callibrated blade, a metal stock and a set 45°. One of 150 mm (6 in) blade length is recommended for general use. For marking across the grain prior to saw-cutting, a marking knife is useful. Craft knives with thin blades and metal handles are not ideal for this work, for slightly thicker blades give clearer lines. Where tenon shoulders are angled a sliding bevel will allow for smooth action of the marking knife.

When marking for mortises and tenons, a mortise gauge is required. Modern ones have a single spur fitted, as well as the twin spurs, so you can gauge single lines along the grain for rebates.

Chisels

Chisels are sharp-edged tools. They are polish-ground during manufacture and should be protected with plastic caps when not in use. As they are all-purpose tools, as wide a range as possible should be kept. The specialist chisels are firmer, bevel edge, mortise and paring. Where the number of chisels is limited it is probably best to mix firmer with bevel edge chisels and have only the most likely sizes for mortising. Plastic handles are more tough than wooden ones and stand up better to driving.

Firmer chisels have square edges, are reasonably heavy and will accept some driving by a mallet – never a hammer. Hammers split the chisel handles and make them rough to hold. Useful sizes of mixed firmer and bevel edge chisels are 6 mm (¼ in), 9 mm (⅜ in), 12 mm (½ in), 18 mm (¾ in), and 25 mm (1 in), with the 6, 12 and 25 mm ones bevel-edged. Bevel edge chisels are bevelled on their edges to enable close paring for intricate work. As far as is reasonably possible, always drive the bevel edge chisel by hand; avoid using a mallet with small sizes.

Mortise chisels

These are long and strong and their handles are designed for mallet-driving. Since you should always make a mortise the exact width of a chisel, the chisels are used as a guide for the width setting of the two mortise gauge points. They are made to a nominal size; since they are polished with an abrasive belt in the factory, no accurate size is certain. Two 9 mm (⅜ in) mortise chisels may well vary by 0.4 mm ¹⁄₆₄ in).

8

They should be held upright, driven into the marked mortise position and worked along, the bevel being reversed at half-way. They should not be used like garden spades digging their way into a trench.

Making a mortise

There are several ways of doing this, so by trial and error find the method that suits you. The correct method is to stand facing the end of the piece of wood to be mortised, which should be firmly held with plenty of packing beneath to absorb the blows. Hold the chisel upright in the centre of the mortise, bevel towards you. Drive in with the mallet. Re-site the chisel, this time closer to you, and drive again. The bevel will drive the chisel forward as you knock it down. This action shears the sides of the chips in front of the chisel. Re-site the chisel nearer to you again and proceed.

When the chisel reaches within 0.8 mm (1/32 in) of the nearest end line, reverse the bevel of the chisel, start again at the centre and work out. When close to the other end line, start again in the centre. Gradually the hole will deepen. Remove cut chips with a very careful digging/shovelling action, but do not lever on the mortise ends.

When the centre is clear, position the chisel upright again, bevel in towards the centre just inside the nearest mortise-end line. Strike down and the bevel will drive the chisel back to the line as it cuts down. Repeat for other end.

If a through mortise is required, cut to half the depth and turn the wood over. Repeat the process until the mortise is clear – and is a neat rectangular slot.

Other chisels

The paring chisel is a long, thin, wide and bevelled chisel used for paring away by virtue of its sharp wide edge. It is not a tool for unskilled use.

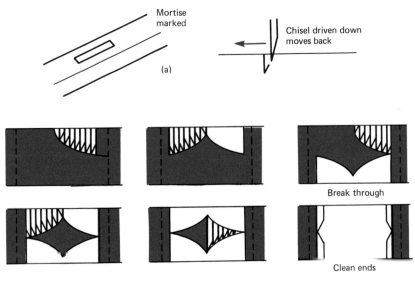

Marking a mortise, and progressive chopping

For really heavy chiselling, extra strong firmer chisels are made that have a shouldered tang (the bit that goes into the handle) and a handle that has ferrules (the metallic ring round most tool handles) at both ends. These tools, which may be driven very heavily, are called registered chisels.

Hammers

The two main woodworkers' hammers are the Warrington and the claw. These are sold in weight sizes. The points to look for when purchasing are that the heads are firmly attached with either firmly glued, wooden wedges or barbed, metallic wedges, driven in at an angle to the end grain, and that the handle haft, or shaft, as it is variously called, is of light

Other hand tools, and tools you can make yourself

coloured hardwood and straight grained. Hammer handles are best made of ash or hickory, for both these woods are very strong and shock-absorbent. Steel shafts are stronger, but expensive. For general work the 340 g (12 oz) Warrington (No 2) is recommended, being neither too light nor too heavy. The claw hammer (No 4½) is useful for heavy driving and for extracting nails. A reasonable weight is 450 g (16 oz).

A light, slim-section Warrington on a slender handle is called a pin hammer. This is exceptionally useful for fine pinning or for driving in glazing sprigs.

Other tools

The remaining tools on the list shown on page 2 are so general that most people should be familiar with them. The cork

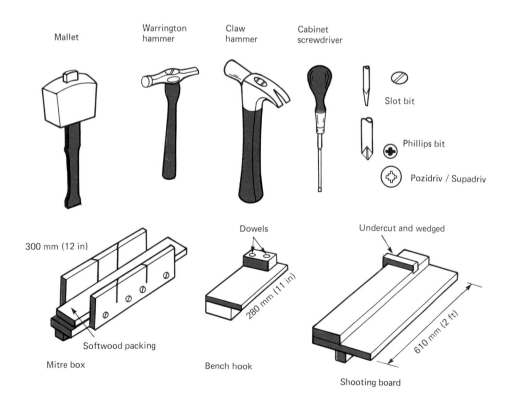

Mallet

Warrington hammer

Claw hammer

Cabinet screwdriver

Slot bit

Phillips bit

Pozidriv / Supadriv

300 mm (12 in)

Softwood packing

Mitre box

Dowels

280 mm (11 in)

Bench hook

Undercut and wedged

610 mm (2 ft)

Shooting board

sanding block is used because its surface is resilient enough to be gentle in action when it is used to back up sandpaper (abrasive paper).

Twist drills are small-size drills with straight shanks for use in the wheel brace or electric drill. Jennings bits (twist drills) have square shanks to fit the hand brace and, normally, threaded centres at the end to help pull them into the wood.

The wheel brace is the one with a hand-rotated gear wheel to turn the drill. The hand brace has a cranked centre section for hand-swinging.

Then there are pincers, a nail set or punch and screwdrivers. The most useful screwdriver is the 150 mm (6 in) cabinet screwdriver, which has a bulbous handle that is easily gripped. Smaller drivers are very useful, together with a starred-bit (cross-slot) type to drive Pozidriv screws. The screwdriver length is measured from bit end to tang ferrule.

A block-sharpening stone of medium grade must be an early purchase.

Self-made tools

The first project should be the bench hook, for this provides a working place and support for many cutting jobs. Shoulder cuts for tenons and housings are made on it; small items may be rested on it for paring down with chisels; and it provides a solid, horizontal stop, should you wish to knock out a tenon from a tight mortise.

The bench hook consists of a flat beech board approximately 275 mm (11 in) long by 150 mm (6 in) wide and 22 mm (⅞ in) thick. Any stable piece of wood will do,

but beech provides good strength and durability. Two end stops are cut square and cramped across while dowel holes are made. The dowels are then glued and driven in; screws would damage sharp tools.

Mitre cuts for framing mouldings are best made in a mitre box, which is an open-topped, open-ended box. This again should be in beech, with the sides and base being 18 mm (¾ in) thick. The sides are screwed into the base and the ends cut very square. Careful measurement and marking will give the positions for the two cuts at 45° across. These should not go down to the base for reasons of strength; the mouldings being cut are supported on a replaceable base piece of wood. The side cuts are made with the same tenon saw used for the mitres.

To enable edge and end-planing of small pieces (chessboard squares, for example) and of longer edges of material too thin to be held upright in the vice, a shooting board is a must.

The shooting board is held in a vice by the bottom piece screwed up to its lower side or, if a bench stop is available, simply pushed against this stop. The work piece is held firmly against the stop notched into the board and a steel plane, nicely sharp, is rapidly pushed along the board, enabling a fine shaving to be taken. The board end stop is set square to the board edge at its front edge. The back edge of the stop is tapered in length and in height. The housing across the board is tapered to suit the stop. Thus, when the stop is driven in, it is securely held. After a period of use the front end of the stop wears; if it is knocked out and a shaving removed from one side, it may be knocked in again with its front end levelled with the board edge.

On completion, all wooden workshop tools should be given protective coatings of raw linseed oil.

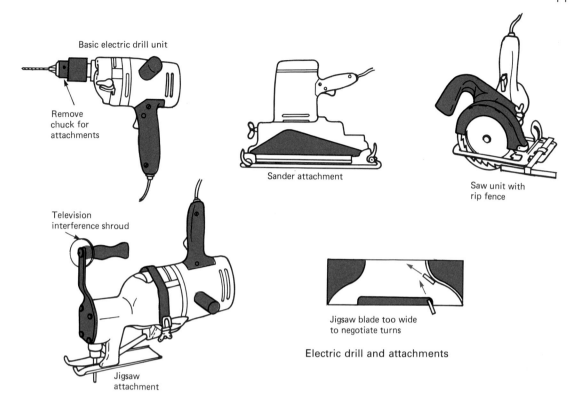

Basic electric drill unit

Remove
chuck for
attachments

Television
interference shroud

Jigsaw
attachment

Sander attachment

Saw unit with
rip fence

Jigsaw blade too wide
to negotiate turns

Electric drill and attachments

Power tools

Start with a hammer drill with as large a chuck size as you can afford – 9 mm (⅜ in) is sufficient for most home jobs. Two-speed or variable speed drive is an essential, for when attachments are added slower speeds are sometimes required. For wall-drilling with carbide-tipped bits this slow speed is also essential.

The most useful attachment is the saw unit, especially if you can afford a carbide-tipped circular saw which will cut melamine-faced chipboard cleanly and easily. You may also find other attachments useful.

Sanding

Sanding is hard work and any help electric tools can give should be welcomed. The orbital sanding attachment will enable finish-sanding. It will not take really rough work down to polishing smoothness; but once the main visual imperfections have been planed or hand-sanded away, the orbital sander will happily take over – if you are prepared to go down through several grades of abrasive paper. In short, start coarse, change to medium and finish smooth.

The drill itself may be used as a sanding aid if some of the variety of sanding heads available are bought. The sanding drum, which is a medium/dense foam disc, has an abrasive-coated, linen sleeve pressed on to it. It is useful on square or shaped edges where the curvature is not too great. The flapwheel consists of a tightly packed drum of abrasive-coated, linen flaps, and is intended for use on curved edges and nosed mouldings. With the flat discs that fit on to the drill chuck, self-adhesive abrasive discs may be used and simply peeled off when worn out.

As with all sanding, do not expect something for nothing. Smooth in stages and finish finally when the rough has been taken down to smooth.

Jigsaw

This attachment has limited use, but like the sander it works well if sensibly used and saws are correctly selected. In use it should be fed only so fast as it wants to cut. Bends should be negotiated at the will of the saw; if the blade does not want to go round, it is too wide. Change the blade to suit the job.

The value of the jigsaw will depend entirely on its user. Treat it carefully and use it within its limits, and it will prove invaluable. Force it and try to make it do work beyond its capacity, and it will soon be relegated to a box under the bench.

Drill base

This is a horizontal holding frame for the electric drill. Its main purpose is when the drill is to be used as a small lathe, and for the attachment of a grinding wheel unit. The grinding wheel unit enables chisels and other tools to be serviced.

Purpose-made units

Purpose-made electric tools have more power and are much easier to handle than drill-and-attachment kits. The initial expense is higher, but time is saved on each operation because the tool is immediately available – unlike those previously described which are inevitably set up for the wrong use when required for a job.

Chapter 2 Choosing materials

The first stage in any woodworking job is to decide what type of wood or board you want to use. Depending on the project in hand, some will be more or less suitable than others. Here is a guide to the merits and limitations of a range of timber and boards you are most likely to want to use.

Softwoods

Softwoods are not necessary soft, neither are hardwoods all hard. Do not go by name and description. Choose the wood for the job by sight and feel. If it feels right and does not show wild, woolly grain with a gummy surface, it should be all right. Avoid sharp, brittle edges; these indicate hard, dense and brittle timber, which will cause you trouble.

Redwoods

The most popular softwoods for home carpentry are known as redwoods, because they have red bark when they grow. They are yellow-to-cream in colour, with whitish sapwood. Any knots are brown-to-golden and usually firmly fixed into the surrounding wood.

Redwoods plane easily to a smooth shiny surface. They also saw and chop very well. They stand without warping, will take nails and screws and paint easily. Use redwoods for all of the non-demanding furniture jobs and for all painted structures.

Douglas fir

This is a popular redwood, but is not that easily worked. It is sometimes called oregon or columbian pine. It is salmon pink in colour with frequent, large, loose knots. As it ages, the knots tend to become slightly raised above the surface. Its working qualities vary, for it is brittle and hard. If carefully selected and worked, it will finish very well and is most attractive for naturally finished furniture. On drying in centrally heated premises, however, it splits easily.

Spruce

Spruce is a woolly softwood, spongy in places and hard in others. It is dead white in colour ('dead' here means lifeless with no sparkle, not the 'dead' white of brilliant white). It comes in wide boards or as timber roofing members.

Spruce works reasonably easily, but its knots tend to be loose and fall out. The knots are bright gold or dark purple to black. The wood tends to be sticky, for most boards have 'rind galls', which are resin pockets. It paints well if the knots are 'knotted' (see page 72).

Hemlock

Hemlock is often called fir. Coarse, woolly, brittle and spiteful, it splinters and

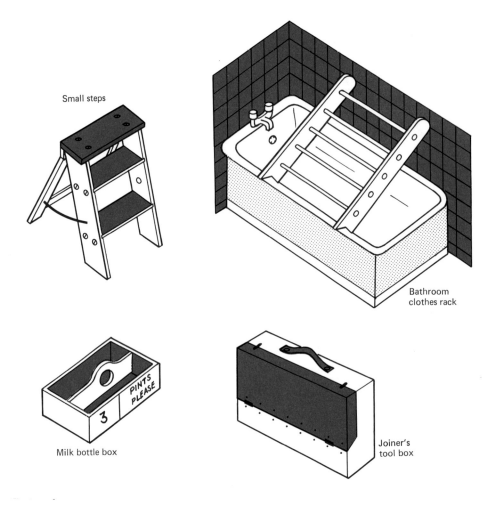

Small steps

Bathroom
clothes rack

Milk bottle box

PINTS
PLEASE

3

Joiner's
tool box

Selected uses of softwood

splits and needs very careful handling and working. It is, nevertheless, suitable for most structural jobs. It is dull pink to light brown in colour, with large dead and black knots. Many imported doors are made of hemlock, for the best boards are sorted out for door joinery before the remainder is marketed as general timber.

Parana pine

This is a fine softwood, clear in length and pure in colour, ranging from yellow to brown, with very strong, red streaks. When yellow, it glows with pride when worked with a sharp tool; when brown, it remains dull and dismal. It works well for all joinery and furniture, taking paint, polish and stain. There is one snag, however; it will not stand still and will turn at the slightest whim.

It is the most suitable of all softwoods indoors, but dislikes the outside so much that it rots away quickly. However, planed and joined well, and brought quickly into cramp, it is most useful. But never trust it overnight; plane it, shape it, joint it and get it into cramps before leaving it.

Some of the uses of selected softwoods are shown in the accompanying drawing.

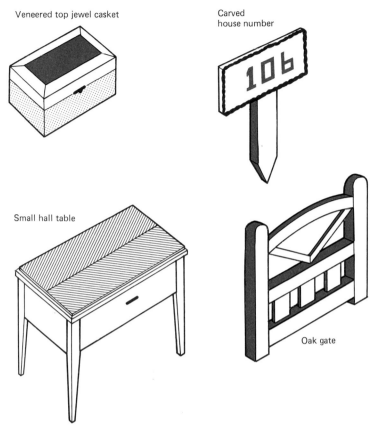

Veneered top jewel casket

Carved
house number

Small hall table

Oak gate

Selected uses of hardwood

Hardwoods

Hardwoods are mostly hard, although some are softer than soft – balsa and obeche, for example. The attractions of hardwoods lie in their ability to stand firm, shape and shine well and to withstand any manner of assault by tools. They must, however, be chosen well for the job in hand. Some are best left in large sections; others may be cut fine. Make sure the colour looks right for the job and the grain is reasonably straight. Beware of hardwoods that are sold as teak type, mahogany type, etc. Many woods have a similar colour to the favourites, but in no other characteristic are they the same.

Oak

Oak will do most things for you. It will remain flat and cuts and smoothes well. It glues and polishes very well and it can be used for fine and fancy shapes as well as in strong and sturdy sections. Fixing it is easy, but never use steel screws; the iron in the screws rots the oak and the acid in the oak rots the screws. Use brass or galvanised steel screws instead.

Oak varies through all shades of brown, sometimes with a slightly reddish tint. For home-working Japanese oak is best. It is a regular brown in colour, consistent in texture and reasonably easy to work with sharp tools. English oak is the most attractive, with a more golden brown than the Japanese. It has very attractive grain configuration, but it also has many knots. American oak may be brown or red, the red being a pink-brown rather than a true brown. Both English and American are reasonably easy to work, although they are not so mild as Japanese oak. Some typical oak jobs are shown in the drawing.

Beech

This is by far the most popular of the hardwoods for general use. In its natural sawn state it is white to pink; but as it is so hard and tough, most of it is steamed. This steaming turns the white to an attractive pink and the hardness to mildness.

Beech is free from most defects and potential hazards. It will plane and saw easily. It is strong and will make strong joints. It will also sand very smooth and take most stains and finishes.

As a furniture wood its appearance is poor, for it has no natural grain features. But as it stains well, it will produce acceptable oak, walnut and mahogany-type furniture. It must never be used out-of-doors, however; it degrades quickly and drastically.

Ramin

This is tropical hardwood, yellow to cream in colour and brittle to use. It is, however, a valuable wood despite its propensity to split when used in small sections. It cuts and smooths well and takes all nails and screws. It is very strong and does not move when positioned. It may be stained and polished to look like oak, walnut or mahogany.

Mahogany

Dont be misled here, since most of the red/brown wood offered for sale is not true mahogny; there are many, many close substitutes. True mahogany – Honduras, African or Brazilian – is a good wood to use. A joinery or furniture material, it has a dark, swirling, red/brown

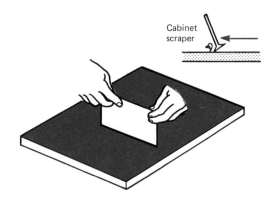

Scraping veneer before sanding

colour with few defects. When of good quality it will stay flat and will smooth well, but may need scraping with a cabinet scraper before sanding.

Utile, sapele, red meranti

All of these look like mahogany and may be sold as mahogany, but they are not. The first two are attractive woods in their own right and are indeed very close to mahogany. They are, however, subject to two main defects. Their grain is interlocked, which means that it lies at all angles to the surface and makes for difficult planing; and, because of their erratic growth (for that is what grain is all about), both are to some extent unstable and will twist if left lying about. Cut them, smooth them, cramp them and, as quickly, seal them.

Red meranti is another wood entirely, although it is red. It is cheese-like to cut, but resinous (gummy) and needs thorough washing with white spirit before staining and finishing. It is reasonably strong and stable and, if stained and finished well, will pass for mahogany if you do not inspect it too closely.

There is a white meranti available that is softer than white beech. Slightly more yellow than ramin, it is useful as a wood for hidden rails and plinths. Sometimes it has small black holes; these are old resin ducts and not worm holes.

Golden walnut

Golden walnut is sometimes found. It is identical to African mahogany apart from its colour, which is golden brown; but it has nothing to do with the walnut family. It is attractive under a clear polish or will appear as mahogany if stained red/brown. It has one unusual feature in that black streaks run end to end.

Teak

Teak is tough, durable, has no knots and works easily and well. Green when first cut, it turns to a golden brown on exposure. One of the most popular and attractive woods for joinery and furniture, it blunts tools quickly, however, and must be glued with synthetic adhesive. To finish teak, use matt finishes such as eggshell polyurethane varnish cut down with fine-grade wire wool and wax, or finish entirely with teak oil, a drying varnish.

General hints

After some practice – and some mistakes – it is usually possible for the home woodworker to exercise reasoned judgement about a piece of wood and its suitability for a particular job. Simple value tests are:

- Is it the right weight?
- Is it the right colour?
- Does it ring if it is tapped with the knuckles?
- Does it lie flat along its length?
- Is it woolly?
- Is it brittle?

Dark, solid woods are heavy and difficult to work. Light-coloured woods should be light in weight; if not, suspect wetness. Most dry woods have a sheen on their planed surface. Some distortion in shape is inevitable, but you will be able to plane it flat and obtain the right size. A dry hardwood will have its own note if knocked; wet (damp) wood has a dull sound. Wet wood feels wet and damp to the cheek and to the palm of the hand. Woolly-grained timber never works well, so ignore it. If the corners pick off into lance-like slivers, the wood is brittle; if it is not otherwise unsuitable, however, the brittleness can be overcome.

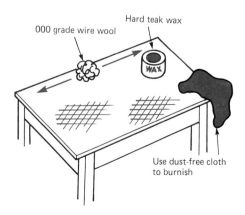

Polishing teak-veneered top

Man-made boards

There is a range of man-made boards of differing compositions. Here is a guide to those most commonly in use for woodwork.

Plywood

This is a board of plies bonded together, each layer having its grain alternated, making it very strong for its weight. Ply is made from many varieties of wood, some completely unsuitable for use as timber. The best boards are of Finnish birch, from three-ply up to multi-ply 25 mm (1 in) thick.

This board never warps, smells pleasantly and works well. It is light yellow to cream in colour and has all its laminations of equal thickness. It is very expensive, so choose it only for quality jobs such as hobbycraft models, visible panels in furniture and in end and door panels in kitchen units, if they are to be painted.

The cheaper plywoods can be any colour from light yellow to dark brown. Almost all are defective in strength because the centre laminate (veneer) is much thicker than the outside veneer. The two faces are of more expensive wood than the core and are sometimes a different colour. Check the edges; if these are splintering and ragged and if the board bends easily, it will not stand on its own and will need rigid support. Use it only for hidden panels, backs or bottoms.

For garden shelters use resin-bonded ply, called WBP (water and boil-proof). This is made of Douglas fir and is a popular building sheet board.

Blockboard

Blockboard is a board made up of narrow strips of wood packed together in width and glued together by having surface skins of veneer bonded to each side. It tends to be lighter than plywood, thickness for thickness, but varies in quality according to the species of timber used in the core. It stays reasonably flat and is suitable for most solid panel jobs. It has, however, been rather pushed out by the modern chipboards.

Variations on blockboard are batten board and laminboard. In the first the woodstrip is used as a core up to 75 mm (3 in) wide. The strips have grooves machined into their faces before assembly to cripple them against twisting and turning. Laminboard has its core made up of thin 4 mm (5/32 in) strips all laid on edge, face to face. It is the best of all man-made boards for stability and general strength to weight ratio. Being very expensive it should be used only for jobs that must stay flat.

Sections of the above boards are shown here.

Particle board (chipboard)

This is a woodchip board, so let us call it that – chipboard. It is made of pre-cut wood chips glued and press-bonded together. There are many qualities and these vary in weight to surface area ratio.

The main three chipboards are extruded board, layerboard and flooring board. The first, if looked at on edge, has its chips packed layer on layer, face to face, row after row, facing towards the end of the board. This is not a suitable one-off-job board. Discard it.

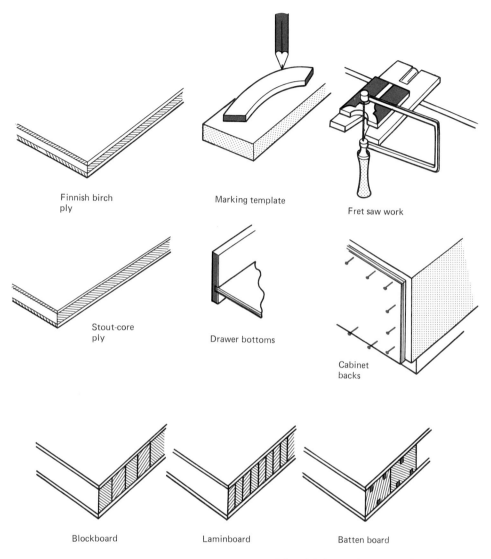

Finnish birch ply

Marking template

Fret saw work

Stout-core ply

Drawer bottoms

Cabinet backs

Blockboard

Laminboard

Batten board

Man-made boards

Layer board is the most popular. It has large-sized chips loosely bonded in its centre and then skin faces of small chips to form surface coatings. It is strong, light, holds screws and is easily cut and shaped.

Flooring board is heavy and dense. Its chips are all indiscriminately packed and it has a higher resin content to give wear resistance and strength.

Sections through each of these boards are shown here.

All chipboards are abrasive to tools, blunting them far faster than natural timber.

Custom board

This board is made of pulped wood fibre similar in many ways to normal standard hardboard. It is made in 12 mm (½ in), 15 mm (⅝ in) and 18 mm (¾ in) thicknesses. It stays flat, may be worked with normal woodworking tools and will take

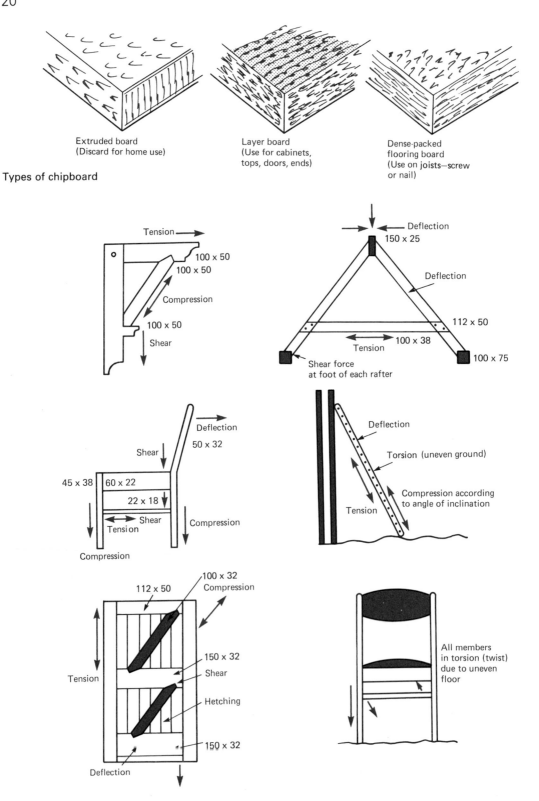

Extruded board
(Discard for home use)

Layer board
(Use for cabinets,
tops, doors, ends)

Dense-packed
flooring board
(Use on joists—screw
or nail)

Types of chipboard

Tension ⟶

100 x 50
100 x 50

Compression

100 x 50

Shear

Deflection
150 x 25

Deflection

112 x 50

Tension ⟵ 100 x 38 ⟶

100 x 75

Shear force
at foot of each rafter

Deflection
50 x 32

Shear

45 x 38 | 60 x 22

22 x 18

Shear
Tension

Compression

Compression

Deflection

Torsion (uneven ground)

Compression according
to angle of inclination

Tension

100 x 32
Compression

112 x 50

150 x 32
Shear

Hetching

Tension

150 x 32

Deflection

All members
in torsion (twist)
due to uneven
floor

Stresses in framed woodwork

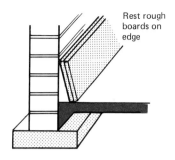

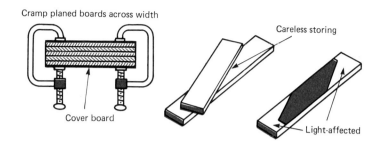

Storage of timber

edge moulding. Edges may be stained and polished without further embellishment. It is lighter than normal hardboard, thickness for thickness, but has one fault; it bruises if knocked. Custom board is not widely available yet, but is used in the furniture industry for dining and reproduction table tops under veneer or leather lay-on.

Approach to using wood

Having decided on a project, decide on the wood. Where chipboard may be used for flat areas, use it; it is simple and easy to handle and has most of the requisite properties. Where structural rails are required, relate their strength requirements to their cross-sections. A non-seen, low-load rail could be of clean, second-hand timber, new softwood or low-cost hardwood, since the roughness of grain and surface finish will not matter.

On the question of structural capacity, base all sizes on existing articles that can be seen. The new woodworker tends to use very much oversized sections. A word of caution. Factory products will in general have better fitting joints than those made at home and may have been made of the smallest section components that would support the job for a limited life.

So use common sense, but remember that most furniture of the cabinet type is now made of chipboard. Chipboard calls for the most exact marking and cutting. All edges must be square and flat for chipboard constructions because they rely on either knock-down (KD) fittings or dowel inserts to pull them square and rigid. Hand-sawing of chipboard rarely produces edges good enough to joint. Power-sawing is the answer.

Look for the type of load. Table legs carry end-on compressive loads. The rails are subject to torsion, shear and tension (twist, side load and pull). As wood will carry high compressive loading, subject to its cross-section giving sufficient stiffness, legs may usually be made much smaller in cross-section than at first thought necessary. The strength of a rail usually depends on the effectiveness of its end joints.

All-in-all, use sensible size timber and, if in doubt, use the next size down. Several of the various loadings applied to wood structures are shown and suggested sizes indicated here.

Keep all boards flat. If timber is bought rough, keep it edge down and carefully propped; flat down, it may absorb water from the floor. Once it is planed, cramp material together between each work session and, especially with hardwoods that are to be polished, protect planed surfaces from light. Two pieces of mahogany placed down roughly with perhaps an edge or end of one piece showing will be subject to patches of light and will darken after only a few days.

Chapter 3 Fittings and fixings

Generally, things that are fixed are called fittings and the things that hold them in place are fixings. In the home the most common base for fixings is the wall – concrete or brick, plasterboard or wood panel. In this chapter fixing to walls and to other bases is covered, together with representative examples of the fixings and methods required. Some of the fittings most frequently met with are also introduced.

Brick walls

Included with brick are all the common wall-building materials, such as aggregate blocks of blue-grey colour, cinder like to the touch; these are called breezeblocks. Aggregate blocks of lighter weight, and of much lighter grey colour, are called light-weight aggregate blocks. You can nail or plug and screw into these.

Bricks need holes, for even the hard drive-in masonry nails find bricks difficult. For secure fixing to brickwork use standard insert plugs and woodscrews.

Drills the hole to the plug size, be it a fibre Rawlplug or a plastic plug. Drive the plug top below the wall surface and open the plug hole with a large nail before screwing. (Plastic one-off plugs have small collars and are driven flush to the brick.)

Holes are difficult to make in concrete; but if a masonry drill (tungsten carbide tipped – TCT) is used in a hammer drill at low speed, usually the hole can be made. Should a exceptionally hard stone be met, split it with an old-fashioned jumper bit driven by a hammer. Steady, regular taps are better than vigorous striking blows, for it is always possible to knock a complete edge off a window lintel. Once the stone is cracked the hammer drill may take over.

Hollow walls

These are mainly stud partitions – sawn timber studs (uprights) with horizontal

Types of wall fixing

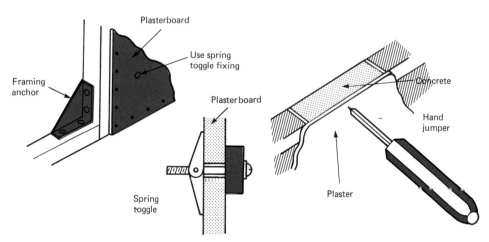

Plasterboard

Use spring toggle fixing

Framing anchor

Plasterboard

Spring toggle

Concrete

Hand jumper

Plaster

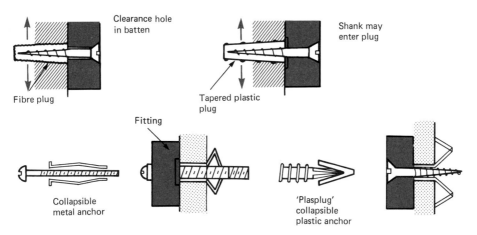

Types of wall fixing

pieces variously called heads, plates and noggings. The frame is then covered with plasterboard. To obtain a secure fixing, first bang with the side of the fist to locate the studs. Having located each upright, tap with the end of a hammer handle to give positive location, but beware of damaging the wall. It is then a simple matter to use woodscrews or nails for fixing. If fixing must be achieved between studs, special fixing are required, as shown in the drawing.

General wood fixings

The most common fixings are nails. Each nail type has its own special job, but each will hold in many situations.

Nail types are: wire nails, which are round and flat-headed; oval nails, which are oval in section with small oval heads; flooring nails (cut brads), which are flat, coarse-looking nails with shouldered heads, panel pins, which are fine round nails of smaller size, with heads small enough to be driven into, and lost in, the wood; veneer pins, which are finer and shorter versions of the panel pin; a large version of the panel pin sometimes found is called the lost head, for although it is

about the same size as its equivalent wire nail, it has a small head that can be easily lost by knocking it flat into the surface; hardboard pins are short, 18 mm (¾ in), square in section, with a very small head, coppered to prevent rust and driven flush into hardboard where they are not easily seen; star nails (not easy to obtain) are driven right through mortise and tenon joints and are lost under paint.

Using nails

Choose the right length of nail, which is usually about twice as long as the thickness of the piece you are fixing. Drive in straight unless you are aiming for extra security, when you angle the nails to each other to form a dovetailed holding. When nailing is done to ends or edges, first blunt the nail with a hammer; it then punches its way through rather than insinuating itself between grain layers. These and other nailing methods are shown here.

Screws

Standard bright mild steel woodscrews are common enough to need no explanation, but there are several points that the

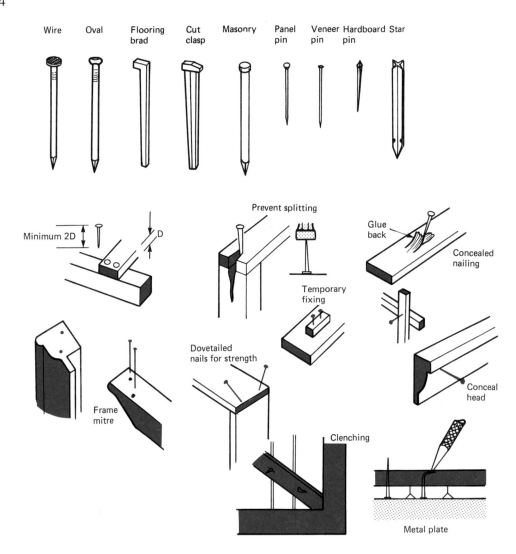

Wire   Oval   Flooring brad   Cut clasp   Masonry   Panel pin   Veneer pin   Hardboard pin   Star pin

Minimum 2D

D

Prevent splitting

Glue back

Concealed nailing

Temporary fixing

Dovetailed nails for strength

Frame mitre

Conceal head

Clenching

Metal plate

Nail types and techniques

non-trade user sometimes overlooks. The number preceding the screw is its diameter code; a No 8 screw has a plain shank of about 4 mm ($\frac{5}{32}$ in), a No 10 about 4.8 mm ($\frac{3}{16}$ in). The higher the number, the thicker the screw. The value that follows the number indicates the length and these are still given in imperial sizes, although some special screws have metric lengths. Numbers 4, 6, 8 and 10 cover most uses with the 12 and 14 being reserved for heavy carpentry. Numbers 2 and 3 are available, but need looking for.

Screws may have slotted heads or starred heads (cross-slots). The slotted head screws must be put in with a screwdriver that fits the slot, otherwise the head will burr and screw splinters will hook into fingers brushed across them. The starred heads are either Pozidriv or Phillips (now obsolete). These give a more positive grip than the slotted type and were really developed for power-driven industrial drivers. Screw head types are shown here.

The threaded portion of a screw should, as far as possible, pass clear through the material to be fixed. Despite the extra trouble of pre-drilling, it is always worth

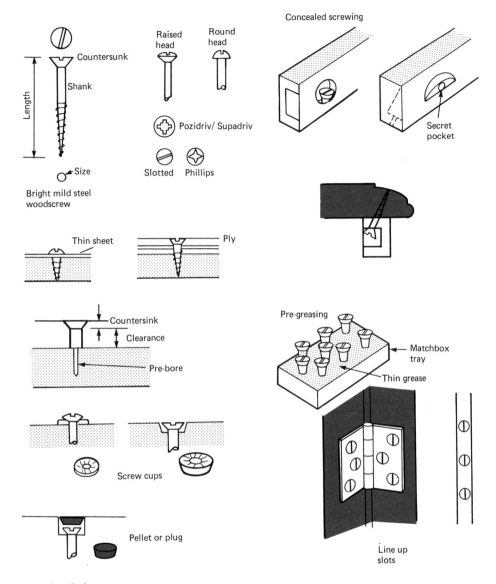

Screw types and techniques

Screw types

the effort. Do not be tempted to drive a screw with a hammer. This can crack the head and leave a partially projecting screw with no means of extraction. Furthermore, hammering shears the wood grain, which would otherwise hold in the screw. Another fault with hammering is that it will lead to latent splits along the wood grain, which develop later as any load is applied. Screwing uses are shown here.

Wood screws are made mainly from mild steel and may be protected from corrosion by platings of brass, cadmium or zinc. Some copper or antique platings may be found in the smaller sizes. Platings are necessary to prevent plain oxidizing (rust) or to prevent the common iron/tannic acid reaction found when steel is driven into oak, when the screw corrodes and the oak rots. Never use steel screws in oak.

If using brass-plated screws, be extra careful of burring the drive slot, for this will lead to corrosion and unsightliness. Solid brass screws are soft and must always be inserted into pre-drilled holes. If used on hardwoods, pre-drill and drive in a steel screw first to open the hole.

Screw heads vary. Most are flat and are countersunk below, but others may be partially raised for appearance or be fully raised and rounded without countersinking. These fully rounded screws are usually black and are called black jappaned screws; they are used to fix exposed fittings that are blacked against the weather. Beware of burring, since immediate rust follows.

Chipboard screws

These are slotted or starred (cross-slots) and have no clear shank. They are parallel and not tapered and normally need no pilot hole other than that made with a bradawl. Their threads may be single or double-start. If double-start, they have a

Double-start   Single-start

Chipboard screws

much higher helix angle, which means that for each revolution of the driver they go in twice as far as single-start screws. Their design is demanded by the loosely packed nature of chipboard. They grip very well and may be used in solid wood, but need a pre-drilled hole in very hard woods.

Choose the right size. The shank must not be too thick for the width into which it is screwed, neither must it be too thin for the load it must carry. Cleanly driven No 8s or 10s will carry most loads; it is the length that counts.

The screw length must be more than sufficient to clear the rear of the material being fixed and must project well in the wall. When plugging, try to arrange for the plain shank to enter the wall but not to enter the plug.

Pre-drill for all long screws (ideally for all screws) and give long thick screws a light coating of grease before driving.

If fixing to ceramic (glazed) tiles, the screw shank must always penetrate beyond the tile and into the base wall. The plug, if it is fibrous or plastic, must be punched in clear of the tile; the tile will crack if the plug is left flush with the tile surface.

When marking for drilling into tiles, lay on a cross of masking tape and make the hole centre on this; otherwise the tungsten drill bit tends to skid across the glaze. An alternative trade trick is to place the point of the bit on the marked spot of an untaped tile and to rotate it forward and backward by hand before drilling. This cuts a shallow centre hole for the bit to bed into, rather like the centre-punching of metal.

The appearance of any screwed job, even hinges, is improved if all the head slots of slotted screws are lined up as they are finally driven.

Mis-marked screw holes may be bradawled down their sides to enable a screw to move slightly sideways. For bad mis-marking in wood, glue in a small plug and start again. For mis-marked holes in walls, lever the existing plug to one side using a heavy nail, insert a slightly smaller plug and rescrew. Alternatively, drive slivers of wood down the plug sides.

Chipboard fittings

Chipboard fittings may be divided into three groups. There are those that do the job that joints do in solid wood, ie holding the parts together. There are those that serve an essentially functional purpose and also those that serve a part-decorative and part-functional purpose. Examples of the first group are two-block knock-down (KD) fittings and nylon screw inserts. Examples of the second group are magnetic catches and shelf supports, and of the third group there are door knobs and metallic (stainless steel or aluminium) door edges or drawer pulls.

Knock-down fittings

The most popular and simple to use are the two-block type. Two interlocking blocks are used, with as many pairs as are necessary for the width of the panels to be jointed. They are usually used in the corners of cabinet carcases made from melamine-faced chipboard (sold in panels of standard widths, with pre-edged edges and grain of mahogany, teak or plain white). A music-centre base of 380 mm (15 in) width, for example, will help provide a rigid carcase if two fittings are used at each corner – eight in all.

In use the technique boils down to accurate marking. Examine the blocks and

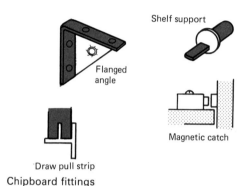

Shelf support

Flanged angle

Magnetic catch

Draw pull strip

Chipboard fittings

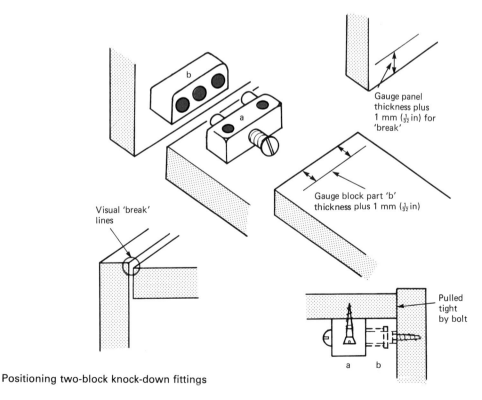

Visual 'break' lines

Gauge panel thickness plus 1 mm ($\frac{1}{32}$ in) for 'break'

Gauge block part 'b' thickness plus 1 mm ($\frac{1}{32}$ in)

Pulled tight by bolt

Positioning two-block knock-down fittings

arrange them so that their locking bolt pulls each corner of the carcase together as it is tightened. Then set a gauge to the width of one block plus 1 mm (1/32 in) and gauge two short lines across the end of the horizontal panel. Use a plywood template to position the correct part of the fitting in from the edges of the panel and screw one chipboard screw only into each part. Treat each end of each horizontal panel. Then re-set the gauge to panel thickness (usually 15 mm) plus one millimetre and gauge across the vertical panels in approximately the correct places. Screw the other block members on with one screw each and knock the unit together. Pull up with the centre bolts. The full method is shown here.

If all is in order, remove the fittings and smear a film of adhesive – PVA or contact – on the base of each block and re-screw them, this time with two screws each. The reason for the adhesive is to prevent slide when tightening the screws. The reason for the 'one screw first' assembly is to allow for the alteration of blocks if incorrectly positioned.

The extra millimetre on the horizontal panel gauging is to give allowance for pulling the blocks together tight. The extra millimetre on the vertical panel gauging is to allow a slight overlap of panels to cover for slight mis-siting of the blocks and to

avoid an unsightly join of panels. This, in the trade, is called a break-line.

Other carcase assembly two-block fittings have tapered interlocks and need no pull-in allowance. They bite together as they are pulled in. These have the trade name 'Plasplug'.

Nylon screw inserts do the same job for carcases, but they are not so strong and need surface buttons to hide the screw

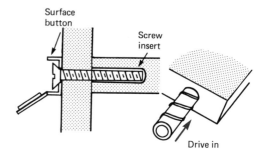

Nylon screw insert

heads. Holes are accurately drilled into the ends of the horizontal panels and the nylon inserts are glued and knocked in. The vertical panel has holes drilled through; screws are then inserted into screw cups and the job is assembled. Four screws would be required on each corner of a 380 mm (15 in) wide panel.

Door catches

Magnetic door catches are simple magnets moulded into a plastic casing. When these fittings are screwed up under a shelf edge or a carcase rail, they attract a keeper plate screwed to the door and, as the door is closed, hold it closed.

When using these, choose a catch large enough for the door to be held. A good rotailer will advise on this and thereafter experience will give you the right size at a glance. Some wide doors will need two or more catches. The wider the door, the

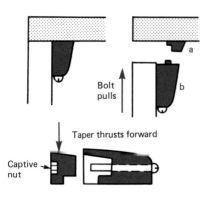

'Plasplug' knock-down fitting

greater its leverage knob to hinge – and the more powerful must be the magnet.

When fitting, place the keeper across the bars of the magnet and position the catch so that the back (door side) of the keeper plate is flush with the rail edge

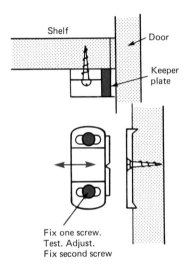

Fix one screw.
Test. Adjust.
Fix second screw

Magnetic door catch

against which the door is to shut. Use a fine-point bradawl to mark the mid-slot position for one of the screws that will hold the block in position; mid-position will give room for slight forward and backward adjustment.

Fix in one screw and close the door. This should push the catch back slightly and align it to the door face. Fix in the other screw. Tap the catch forward slightly and tighten the screws fully. Now, with the keeper plate in its correct position across the magnet, close the door and press against it. When the door is open,

two slight indentations should be seen. Use a bradawl and open each of these to make a very shallow countersunk hole. These shallow holes take the keeper spurs. Centrally between the two holes pre-drill for the keeper plate screw. Fix this plate into position and try the door. If it stands out too much when closed, move the catch back. If it barely holds to the magnet, move the catch forward.

Edging strip

These strips may be purely visual with minimum function or they may operate as drawer or door pulls.

They can be fitted in one of three ways depending on type and size. If the job is light, then contact adhesive may be used, but only if there is no tongue strip. Heavier jobs need the strips drilled, countersunk and screwed in place.

With tongued strip, the chipboard door must be grooved. This is not a practical job if you do not have a thin circular saw run in a drill attachment, or a circular saw unit. Measure the job; set the saw; make a trial cut in an offcut; adjust; check and run the job. If the saw cut is too fine, readjust the saw fence and make a second cut beside the first one.

Sometimes the groove is too wide. If it is, but only by a small margin, try to distort the tongue along its length and then glue it in with Araldite resin adhesive. Another alternative is to glue a veneer strip into the slot before tapping in the edging strip.

Chapter 4
Jointing solid wood and chipboard

Many simple constructions that serve only to carry a load or to provide a frame to which panel cladding may be nailed or screwed may be simply nailed together. Examples of these are one-off casting boxes for concrete, rough bases for fuel containers, stud partitions and, to a large extent, traditional feather-edged board fences. Sometimes, to assist positioning while nailing or to make nailing possible, some notch cuts may be made; but these are not true joints as such.

As the strength and rigidity requirement grows, so the form of the joint must become more complex and be cut with greater accuracy. Two examples show the extremes: the butt and nailed corner of a packing case and the secret mitred and dovetailed corner of a polished hardwood casket. The nailed corner is sufficient in strength once the plywood top and bottom are fixed, whereas the casket will remain jointed forever, with no cramping required on assembly and with no visible sign of support.

The strength of both will rely on the accuracy of the cutting. Even case ends must butt square. Some of the non-cut

Nailed non-cut carcassing joints

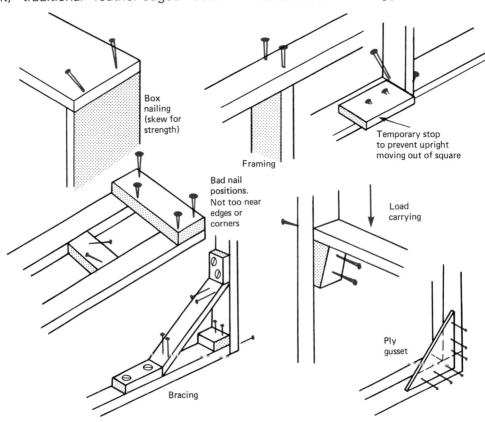

Box nailing (skew for strength)

Framing

Temporary stop to prevent upright moving out of square

Bad nail positions. Not too near edges or corners

Load carrying

Bracing

Ply gusset

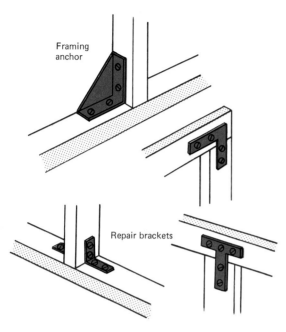

Metal anchors and repair brackets

carcassing joints are shown here. For more permanent fixing, but retaining simplicity, use metal anchors and brackets.

Half-laps

These are saw-cut and either nailed or screwed. There is no strength in the joints other than a minor degree of resistance to triangular distortion. The timber, planed or left rough, is marked with a gauge set to approximately half thickness – both pieces being marked from the same face side (see diagram). When cutting, the saw is fed along the waste side of the line on both pieces so the faces of the two pieces finish flush. When the edges have been gauged, the ends are marked with same setting. If the material has been cut square to length then the gauge is now re-set to the material width and the two opposite faces of the adjoining timbers are marked across. If the ends are not

squared, use a try-square and marking knife. Waste material should be cross-hatched with a pencil and the shoulder cuts squared down to meet the side lines. Cutting is now done.

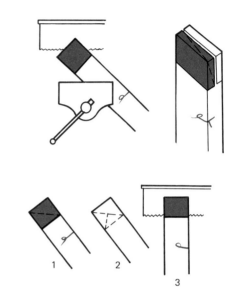

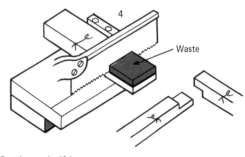

Cutting a half-lap

The marked material (the rail to be cut) is positioned end-up in the vice (see the drawing above), and the saw blade held so that the tooth line is horizontal. The left thumb is used to guide the initial entry of the saw. Keeping the saw in line with the marks, but with its entire cutting thickness (the kerf) to the waste side of the line, the first cut is made. This should penetrate until the cut reaches the short shoulder line on the rail edge and the corner of the end of the rail section. The cut will have covered a diagonal half of the required area to be cut away. At this stage the rail is reversed in the vice and another diagonal cut is made; again keep to the waste side of the line. The saw will drop into the previous cut.

Now position the rail end-up and vertical into the vice. Drop the saw into the previous cut and saw horizontally down to the shoulder line. Treat all pieces of wood in the same manner and then, using the bench hook and the tenon saw, cut down the shoulder lines across each piece until the waste cheek drops free. Chisel away any small irregularities and try all pieces together. When a good fit is achieved, glue and screw or nail.

Housings

These joints provide anchorage against movement but have no resistance to direct pulling unless the housing shoulders are dovetailed under. Housings may be simple notchings or they may be complex, with more than one tongue and with interlocking wedges. Some of the range are shown here.

Housings are marked with a try square, gauge and knife and then the shoulders are cut down with the tenon saw. If the housing is stopped (not run through), a small square mortise is chopped at its inner end. This allows the saw end to run through.

When the shoulder cuts have been made, the material is clamped down for the waste to be cut away. Use a chisel, bevel down, to cut away the waste. As the bevel is down, it drives the chisel up, thus avoiding the risk of over-depth cutting.

Work in from both edges and then finally reverse the chisel and pare away any remaining waste to leave the housing with an accurate flat bottom. Where the wood is tough or where knots lie along the path of the housing, make several saw

Various types of housing

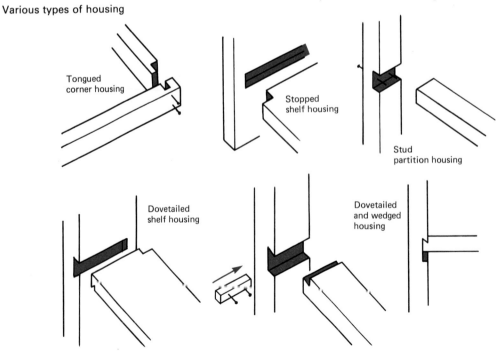

Tongued corner housing

Stopped shelf housing

Stud partition housing

Dovetailed shelf housing

Dovetailed and wedged housing

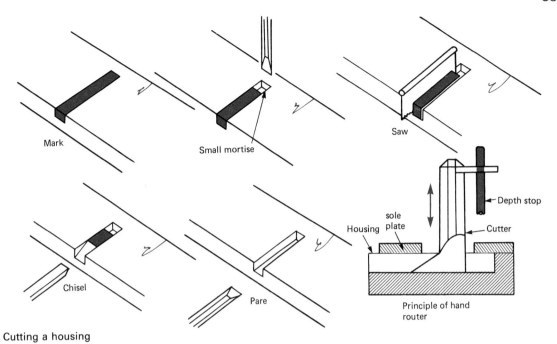

Mark

Small mortise

Saw

Depth stop

sole
plate

Housing

Cutter

Chisel

Pare

Principle of hand
router

Cutting a housing

cuts in addition to the outer shoulders. If the quantity of housings is large and if the work justifies it, a hand router is an ideal tool for flattening the bottoms of the housings.

An electric hand router would of course be able to plough the complete housing.

Mortise and tenon joints

The aim with mortise and tenon joints (as it should be with all joints) is to mark and cut with accuracy so that the tenon will fit from the saw.

When marking, make the tenon thickness as near to one-third the material thickness as possible. Use the next value upwards if in doubt, for thin tenons are weak tenons. If it is necessary to cut back the tenon width for haunchings or because the rail is wide, make the maximum width of tenon approximately three-fifths of the rail width. On very wide rails make two tenons with a haunch in between (cut as one and reduce later).

Choose the chisel and set the mortise gauge to it, for no two chisels are exactly the same width. Use the set mortise gauge to mark both the tenon sizes and mortises. Always use the stock of the gauge on the face side of the material; in the event of uneven material thickness, the two face sides will always come flush. Use a try square and a knife to mark the ends of the mortises and run the set gauge down across the ends of the rails that are to have tenons.

Always use the 'thumb, one, three' rule with the gauge and trail the points by pushing the gauge away from you. Pulling a gauge only works in one situation. If the grain of the wood runs diagonally to the side, it will trap the gauge point and push the stock away. If this happens, try pulling the gauge.

Cutting the mortise

It makes no difference whether the mortise or the tenon is cut first. Work to the lines, chiselling up to the lines, but with the saw skimming the lines on the waste side.

When cutting mortises (see page 8), cramp the material firmly down to a solid bench; vice-cramping will only do for light mortising. Stand facing the end of the work and hold the chisel vertical and square to the rail edge. By sighting along the rail edge and the chisel blade, vertical squareness may be assessed. Remember to hit the chisel with a mallet. Start with the chisel bevel towards you and make the centre cuts first. Work back towards the marked end, making several cuts at each position.

When approaching the end – within 0.8 mm (1/32 in) – stop cutting and reverse the bevel of the chisel. Repeat the operation and clear the waste. Cut again to obtain about half-depth. Turn the rail over, edge to edge, and repeat until the chisel breaks through. Clear the waste by driving a thin wood offcut through. Now line the chisel up vertically and work back to the final mortise end line. Treat all four ends in a similar manner.

Haunches may now be cut, using a tenon saw into the mortise. Clear the waste with a chisel and remove the hairy remnants from the mortise.

If the mortises are large, say for a pair of garage doors, use a suitably sized bit in a hand brace or electrical drill and remove the bulk of the waste before using the chisel.

Cutting the tenon

Mark accurately and always cross-hatch the waste to indicate clearly the waste material.

Using the same process as that described for cutting half-lap joints, cut and remove both tenon cheeks. Carefully clean each shoulder, mark the tenon for any reduction in width and then cut any more waste away. If proper care has been taken, each tenon should now fit each joint. If not, use a wide and sharp chisel to pare excessive tenon thickness gently away. A bullnose plane is preferable to a chisel, but these are expensive.

Remember – and this applies to all woodworking – fit and cramp all joints dry before final gluing; once the adhesive has been spread, adjustment becomes a very messy operation.

Moulded rails

If the frames being made are doors or windows or are for panelling, the cross-sections of the rails will have glass rebates, mouldings or grooves. These are run along the lengths of wood using a rebate plane for the rebates, a plough plane for the grooves and either a moulding plane, electric router or scratch stock for the mouldings.

The rebate plane has it cutting depth set by the adjustable depth stop on its side. The rebate width is set by the fence. In use, the rebate position having been gauged on the wood, the plane is made to start cutting about 150 mm (6 in) from the far end of the length of material. Each cut is started slightly further back along the length until, as the plane is started directly at the nearest end, full depth is almost reached.

The plough or groover is used in the same manner. The electric router is set to the full depth, either for a rebate or groove, and fitted with the correct diameter cutter. If the groove or rebate is very large, or the timber is hard, the cut is set up to be taken progressively.

When using a scratch stock, which looks like a marking gauge with a flat moulded cutter, again start at the far end.

The reason for this information being included here is that each of these tools needs a complete edge for its fence or guide to run along. If the cheek cuts of the tenon are removed before moulding, each of the above tools will fall off at both ends and moulding will be difficult. So, if rails are to be moulded (or in any way re-shaped in section), tenon cheek cuts should be made, but not the shoulder cuts. This leaves the cheeks to support the moulding tools. After the section has been shaped, the shoulder cuts are made.

Dimensions

Frame strength depends both on the accuracy of the joint-cutting and the cross-section of the members compared with the length.

Briefly, the longer the member, the greater its cross-section must be. Rectangular sections tend to be adequate and square sections tend to appear heavy and dumpy. Most structural sections are left rough sawn at about 50 mm (2 in). If they are to carry any load across a span (roof and floor situations) their depth must be sufficient to prevent deflection – 112 mm (4½ in) for light roofs and 175 mm (7 in) or more for floors.

Joinery timbers (for doors and windows) tend to finish at 45 mm (1¾ in), with door stiles being 45 × 95 mm (1¾ × 3¾ in) and window framing (sashes) 32 × 45 mm (1⅜ × 1¾ in).

With furniture, structural members in hardwood rarely finish thicker than 21 mm (⅞ in) and wider than 45 mm (1¾ in); often they are made much lighter. Tenons must be very tight fitting for small hardwood jointing, but can be much easier in fit for large joinery work.

Cutting a rebated tenon

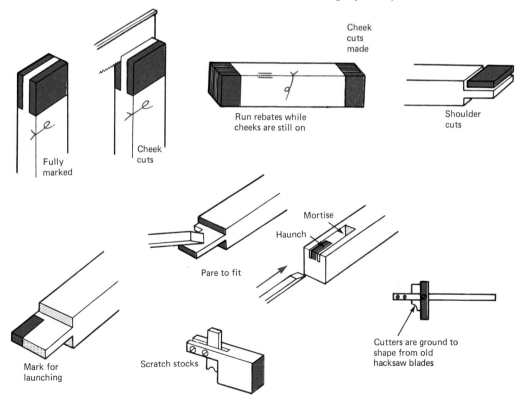

Edge-to-edge jointing

Since the arrival of man-made sheets, solid wood has not been edge-jointed to any great extent. However, it is still sometimes necessary for table tops, box sides and the Scandanavian-look softwood furniture.

Good square-edged jointing, where the adhesive strength is the only strength, relies on very accurate shooting of each board. Shooting means planing an edge straight and square – not an easy task.

If boards to be jointed are bowed out of line in their length, then some mechanical keying is required to hold each board flat with its neighbour while it is being glued. The keys used are dowels, loose tongues, and tongues and grooves.

For natural-finished softwood furniture, dowels are best for they do not show on the ends of the boards, which are normally exposed.

Dowels

Dowelling requires accurate marking, boring, tightly fitting dowels and straight planing of the edges. The same criteria of size is used as with the tenon. A dowel should be approximately one third of the wood thickness in diameter. Linear spacing between dowels will depend on the length of the panel being made and the tendency of wood to warp. Parana pine tends to move much more than deal, so perhaps in a 900 mm (3 ft) length, edge to edge, an extra dowel may be useful – say five in deal, six in parana pine, but only four in red beech.

The dowels themselves are usually of white beech; if bought in long lengths, however, they may be of ramin. Beech dowels are best. There are several patterns of pre-cut dowels on the market that have the ends dubbed to make insertion easier than it would otherwise be; these have their outer skin crushed into a series of reeds. Because crushed wood recovers if moistened, these reeded dowels (which are sold by the packet) swell as they absorb the adhesive and make a good tight joint.

If dowels are cut from a length and they are tight to the hole, there will be no room for air or excess adhesive to be expelled as the dowels are driven home. To overcome this, the short-cut pieces should be rubbed lengthwise along the teeth of a tenon saw so that a small groove is cut in them.

Dowelling

Bore a trial hole in a scrap piece of the same material as the job. Try the dowels into this; a good solid knock should be needed if dowelling hardwood. It is expensive to start with, but dowels must fit tightly. You must buy a drill to fit the nominal size of the dowel and then keep selecting dowels (which vary a lot) until the right number of cut pieces are available.

If good-fitting dowels are not available, make your own. Find, or drill, a hole in a 6 mm (¼ in) piece of steel plate; for most work 9 mm (⅜ in) diameter is sufficient. Cut beech offcuts to 9 mm (⅜ in) square and drive them through the hole; they should then fit the hole bored into the wood.

Cramp the two boards together and square across to make the position points for the dowels. Use a gauge to spur along to make crosses for accurate centres.

Depending on width and other dimensions of the material, bore vertically down

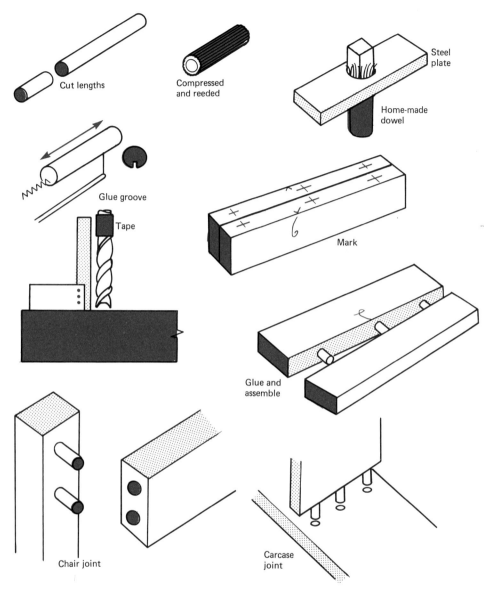

Cut lengths

Compressed and reeded

Steel plate

Home-made dowel

Glue groove

Tape

Mark

Glue and assemble

Chair joint

Carcase joint

Using dowels to make joints

or horizontally in. By eye, or with some-body else's help to keep the boring bit square to the work, bore the right number of holes. Do not go too deep; to avoid this, use a piece of masking tape stuck around the drill bit to give you a depth register.

Knock out the chips, then prepare the cramps. Insert adhesive into the dowel holes with a small stick. Drive in the dowels (it is not usual to dry-test dowel joints, so mark and bore accurately) and coat both joint edges with adhesive. Start at one end and feed each dowel into its correct second hole. Then cramp up. Check for flatness and clean off surplus adhesive.

Other solid wood joints

After half-laps, housings, mortise and tenons, and dowels, there remains only dovetailing and corner-locking. The edge-to-edge joints other than those jointed with dowels are solid tongued and grooved, and those with double grooves and loose ply strips (tongues) to act as keys. Mitres, where pieces meet at angled corners, with or without loose tongues, are simply variations on edge-to-edge butting, where each work face must be flat and true to enable a close butt to be made. Mitres require very clean and accurate cutting.

Making dovetail joints

Dovetails

As the name implies, the key, tongue, tenon or tail of these joints is dovetailed. That is, both edges are tapered towards each other away from the extreme end.

Dovetail cutting is a job calling for very precise marking and cutting. As far as possible, the joint should fit together straight from the saw and require only a sharp mallet blow.

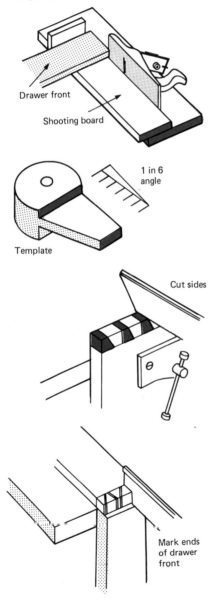

Drawer front

Shooting board

1 in 6 angle

Template

Cut sides

Mark ends of drawer front

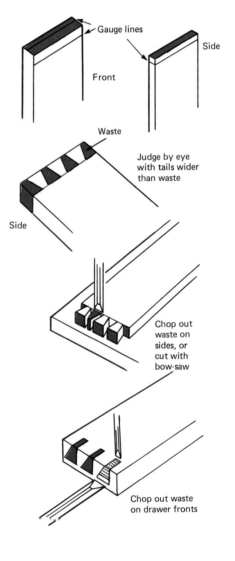

Gauge lines

Front

Side

Waste

Judge by eye with tails wider than waste

Side

Chop out waste on sides, or cut with bow-saw

Chop out waste on drawer fronts

Dovetail joints have many variations (see page 44 and 45). Most common is the drawer dovetail, where drawer sides are dovetailed into the ends of the drawer fronts to form a box. The form of the joint enables the drawer to be pulled out without the sides being pulled from the fronts.

In general, the angle of the shape of the dovetail should be between 1 in 6 and 1 in 8, with the 1 in 8 angle producing the strongest joint. The process to cut a drawer dovetail (and in general most dovetails) is as listed below and step-by-step stages are shown in the diagram.

1. Cut and square (using the shooting board) both the drawer front end and the end of the drawer side.
2. Set a gauge to about three quarters of the drawer front thickness; gauge across the end and also both sides and edges of the drawer side.
3. Set the gauge to the thickness of the drawer side and gauge across the inner face of the drawer front.
4. Mark out the dovetails on both faces of the drawer side, using a simple wooden marking template. Cross-hatch the waste.
5. Place the drawer side end up in the vice and mark the ends of the tails across. Cut down to the shoulder line, keeping the saw very tight to the waste sides of the marked lines.
6. Place the drawer front end up in the vice, with the inner side to the bench; hold the drawer side exactly in place and, with the tip of the saw that has been used to cut the tails, firmly scribe lines across the drawer front end.
7. Chop out the waste between the dovetails on the drawer side, using a narrow chisel and mallet from both sides. If the job is a large one and the tails large, cut out the bulk of the waste with a coping saw before chiselling.

8. Chop out the sockets for the tails in the ends of the drawer front. Use two sizes of chisel. Test and make a finer adjustment where necessary.

Dowelling chipboard

Chipboard cannot be joined using conventional solid wood joints. Once the outer

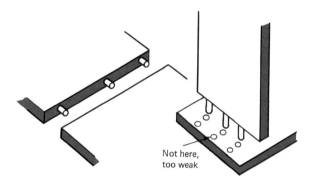

Not here, too weak

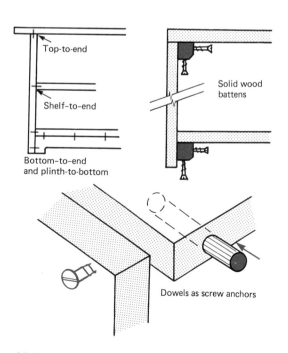

Top-to-end

Shelf-to-end

Bottom-to-end and plinth-to-bottom

Solid wood battens

Dowels as screw anchors

Methods of jointing suitable for chipboard

skin of chipboard has been cut, most of its strength has gone. Thus chipboard jointing involves dowelling or the use of screw-on fittings or strips of solid wood.

Edge-to-edge joints are marked and dowelled in the same way as in solid wood. Owing to the internal weakness of chipboard, make sure that the dowels are not too tight in their holes; it should be possible to just push them in with the fingers.

When using dowels for chipboard carcase construction, mark accurately, bore and assemble; but at no time allow either part of the joint to waver, for this will crack the board. In fact, dowels in chipboard are only locators while the adhesive sets; the true, close-fitting joint between the two accurately cut wood surfaces gives the strength once the adhesive has set.

Dowels, with care, may be used on side-to-end carcase joints, plinth-to-bottom carcase joints and top-to-side and shelf-to-end joints.

Other constructions for chipboard

The strongest joint is the double-screwed batten joint where, at a corner, a strip of solid wood is glued and screwed to both of the chipboard panels. Where these may be unseen, they should be used because they give great strength. Situation such as bottom-to-end, top-to-end, plinth-to-bottom and shelf-to-end are ideal, especially if the cabinet top is below eye level.

Dowels may be used as screw anchors in chipboard and, if desired, as shelf supports.

Methods of firm jointing used in chipboard designs are shown in the diagram.

Chapter 5
Using tools for joint-cutting

Introductory tool usage for joint-cutting was described in Chapter 4. This chapter takes more simple joints, explains how to cut them and suggests situations where they may be used.

Mitres

A mitre is an angled intersection, where two identical wood sections meet with a joint that bisects the total angle. Take the picture frame, for example. Here we have two moulded and rebated sections, each of low strength because of a small overall dimension and each joined strongly to the other and presenting a neat face to the world.

There are joints that may be used for these corners, but they are very intricate in detail and require highly skilled cutting. The mitre, accurately cut and glued, provides a joint acceptable in strength and appearance. However, there are one or two simple tricks that will enable you to strengthen your mitre.

First the mitre. For this you need a mitre box or block. This provides a fence and bed for the material, to support it while it is being cut. The tenon saw used should drop neatly into the sawing slots in the box. If these are worn, then the box needs new sides.

With a rebated moulding, the glass or picture length (if it is for a picture that you are cutting) is marked on the inside faces of the rebate and the moulding is then positioned so that these marks come below the saw blade. However, if the moulding is gilded and ornate, then it will have to be cut mould-up to avoid chipping. Marking will have to be to the overall length, marked on the outside of the moulding.

Measure the moulding thickness from the outside across to the back wall of the rebate. Double this size and add it to the picture size. Add 1.6 mm (1/16 in) for possible out-of-squareness of the glass and mark the outermost corner length on each piece of moulding. Position and cut to these lines.

The four pieces of the frame are now offered together. Any adjustments are made using a shooting board with a mitre stop and a steel smoothing plane. If the job has been carefully cut, no adjustment will be necessary.

Small frames may be left glued, but larger and heavier frames need something more. Support each moulding piece in turn and pin the mitres. This is not as easy as it sounds, so practice on spare bits. Pre-bore for the panel pins to be used; if one piece of the moulding is held padded in the vice, the other piece may be glued and pinned on. Better still, cramp one of the long pieces to a flat board (use plenty of padding on top) and then tap the panel pins into the joint on the shorter piece of moulding. Glue the faces and tap the pins home. Allow possibly 1.6 mm (1/16 in) overlap to allow for the angles to slide as the pins are knocked.

A further mitre-strengthening device is to cut across the corners of the frame and insert veneer feathers, gluing them in. When these feathers are cut and sanded, they tend to look decorative. Another way of strengthening is to use a paper stapler

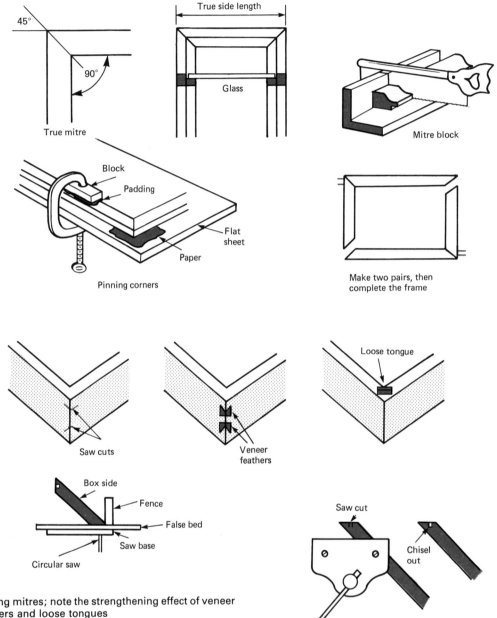

45°

90°

True mitre

True side length

Glass

Mitre block

Block

Padding

Flat sheet

Paper

Pinning corners

Make two pairs, then complete the frame

Saw cuts

Veneer feathers

Loose tongue

Box side

Fence

False bed

Saw base

Circular saw

Saw cut

Chisel out

Making mitres; note the strengthening effect of veneer feathers and loose tongues

on the back across the joints. For heavier joinery-type mitres, loose tongues may be inserted.

To cut for loose tongues (on, perhaps, the sides of a jewellery box), the mitres are cut and tested first. If you have an electric saw, clamp it plate-up in the work vice, using suitable padding. Set the angle to 45° and then cramp on a false bed,

which you have already prepared, with a clearance slot for the saw and a fence to guide the work. The saw should project no more than 3 mm (⅛ in). Feed the box sides in turn over the running saw, using a substantial pushing block.

The loose tongues must be planed to fit the grooves and their width reduced to about 5 mm (³⁄₁₆ in). Test, adjust and glue.

If the grooves must be cut by hand, you need to gauge their position along the mitre face, suiting the gauge setting to a suitable width chisel. Cramp the mitred piece in the vice and use a fine back saw to cut the groove sides. Clean the centre portion away with the narrow chisel and then test, adjust and glue.

Cross-halvings

These are useful for many constructions, including shed-framing, furniture bases, box divisions and carcases.

All cross-halvings need accurate marking and cutting. The two parts are normally identical, but one has the cut-out notch at its top edge and the other has it at the bottom.

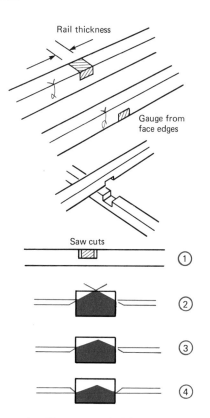

Marking and cutting a cross-halving

The process is to mark out each rail using a try square and a marking knife, carefully keeping the lines as an accurate measure of the material thickness. Square these lines down both faces of each rail and then gauge from line to line, again on both faces.

Now saw down on the waste side of each line and either chop down on the bench top or chop horizontally in the vice.

Tenon variations

There are several variations of the tenon, which you may find helpful to know about, depending on the type of job you are tackling.

Long and short shoulders

Where rebated rails are to meet rebated uprights (stiles), the rail shoulders will need to be off-set and have what are called long- and short-shouldered tenons. Marking is simple. Mark for square shoulders, with the length between shoulders equal to the sight size; this is the width of

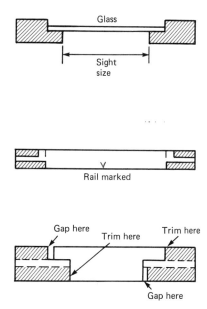

Long- and short-shouldered tenons

44

glass in a frame that you can see through, wood to wood.

Decide the depth of the rebate and then add this at each end to the first shoulder length marked. These two new lines now become the long shoulder and must be on the rebated face of the rail. Mark as described earlier, using a mortise gauge, then make the tenon cheek cuts, but not the shoulder cuts. Run the rebates and then cut the shoulders. Try the tenon into

the stile and adjust the rebate depth, or short-shoulder length, until both shoulders are a good tight fit.

Carcase joints

New wood is not ideal for solid carcases, for the quality of new wood is not what it was. If old timber is available, use it.

Corners are the problem, for these may be joined in secret with no sign of the joint

Dovetails and other corner joints

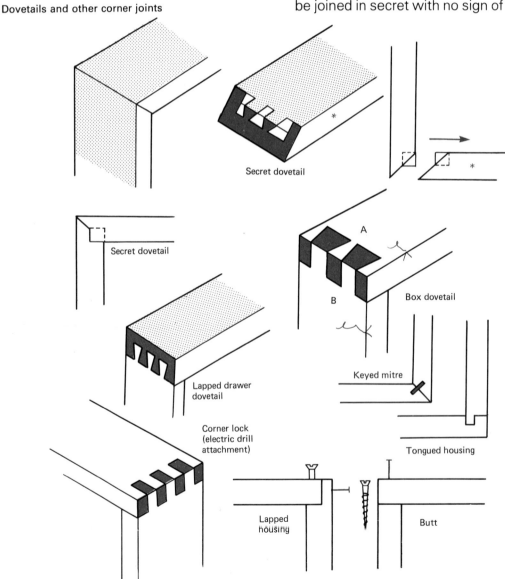

Secret dovetail

Secret dovetail

Box dovetail

A

B

Keyed mitre

Lapped drawer dovetail

Corner lock (electric drill attachment)

Tongued housing

Lapped housing

Butt

showing at all, or they may be joined part-secret with only the indication of a lap-over in sight. The joint may be a plain box dovetail or a straight corner-lock finger joint. Keyed mitres or tongued housings may be used. Straight-lapped housings or butt joints will also make good corner joints, but they need to be pinned or screwed.

All these joints are shown in the diagram.

Corner-joint cutting

Secret dovetails are extremely difficult to cut and are best left until a high degree of skill has been acquired. Basically, as with all dovetailed joints, they rely on accurate marking, cutting and fitting. With dovetails of all types, there is no margin for error; a loose dovetail is loose, and nothing you can do will make it tight.

The secret lapped dovetail is slightly less exacting in cutting, but again it is really a good craftsman's job.

The box dovetail lies within the scope of the home woodworker. Here is the order of working. Square both adjoining ends. Set the marking gauge to the thickness of the wood and lightly gauge all round the ends of both pieces. With a pencil, sketch in the dovetail form (apportion dimensions by eye until they look right) on piece A (see drawing below) and then mark the true outline with the dovetail template (see page 38). Place the piece end-up in the vice and cut down to the base lines, watching both the back and front of the wood as you go. The saw must cut snugly to the waste side of the line.

Change over to piece B and place this in the vice end-up. Lay the piece just cut in the position in which it will finally fit. Drop in the saw tip and score the pattern of the previous saw cuts on to the horizontal end of piece B.

Use the template again to reinforce these score marks, but (and this is a big

Cutting a box dovetail

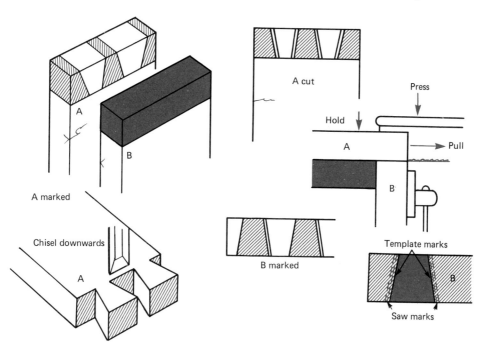

A marked

Chisel downwards

A cut

Hold

Press

Pull

A

B

B marked

Template marks

Saw marks

but) you must allow for the fact that on piece A the waste side of the line will be the opposite to the waste side of the line on piece B. Stop and think, and move the template to its correct position before marking.

Square down from the dovetail socket outlines until the squaring lines meet the gauged lines. Now cut down the lines just drawn.

Use a coping saw to cut out the bulk of the waste on both pieces and finish by using really sharp bevel edge chisels to clean up the outlines of both tails and sockets. Check that the shoulders are square. This cleaning process is done with the two pieces in turn being clamped down flat, on waste wood, to the bench top. Chisel downwards.

Hold piece B in the vice and tap piece A down. If it enters well, keep tapping until the joint is closed. If at any point you feel too much resistance, take the joint apart and slightly ease the high pressure spots; these will show as polished highlights on the cut wood.

Tongued housings

Tongued housings are marked across, working from the pre-squared ends of the two pieces. The tongue should be about one-third of the wood thickness, or as close to this as there is a chisel size available to cut the groove. The depth of the tongue should be about half of the thickness of the board into which it goes.

If at all possible, mark the lines with a cutting gauge, which has a narrow blade cutting edge, rather than with the spur of the marking gauge. It Is used for cross grain marking. The process for the groove is to saw and then to chisel away the waste. if a grooving plane is available with

the right size cutter, use this to clean out the cut groove.

It is always best to leave the grooved board slightly longer than it will finally be, for this allows minor irregularities in the line of the groove to be lost as this additional waste is planed away when the adhesive has set.

The tongue is either saw-cut both ways, saw-cut and chiselled along the grain or made completely with the rebate plane. The final thickness of the tongue is obtained using a shoulder plane.

With these joints, full final fitting must be left to the last before final gluing. This is essential because when sanding to smooth, which is normally the last operation, the tongue is made thinner; so it must be left slightly thick to allow for this and then adjusted after sanding.

Lapped housing

The housed member of this joint is marked with the cutting gauge and then, if a rebate plane is available, housed with this; the final fitting is done with the shoulder plane. An alternative method to this is to saw down the shoulder, cramp on a batten as a fence and plane away

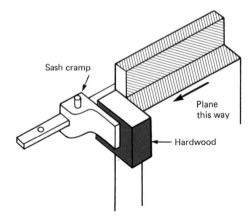

Shoulder-planing a housed end

down to the thickness line with a shoulder plane.

A point to note about the rebate plane is that it has a small spur set into its side. Sharpen this and set it to project below the side of the plane and set the plane fence so that the spur runs in the gauge-cut line.

If the shoulders of either of the last two joints need planing, place them end up in the vice and use the shoulder or bullnose plane to correct them. Cramp a small piece of hardwood across the end of the shoulder to prevent break-out.

Multiple tenons

When two wide boards are joined, both boards should be able to move (shrink) together but with the joint remaining effective. One way to do this is to cut multiple tenons across the joint and to wedge them from outside.

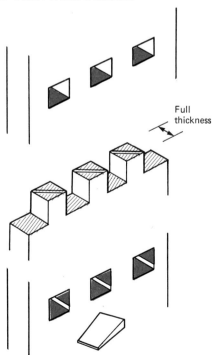

Multiple tenons

The process is to cut one very thick tenon across the full width of one piece and then cut it down into a number of square tenons that run back to the shoulder. If the boards are about the right thickness, leave the tenons full thickness as shown in the diagram.

Mark the mortises to correspond and then bore them right through, boring from both faces to avoid break-out. Fit the tenons and then make a diagonal cut across them. When glued and cramped, a wedge is driven into each tenon and then cut off and sanded flush.

Lap and scarf joints used for lengthening

Sometimes it is necessary to reclaim waste wood or to make use of new wood offcuts by joining pieces together lengthwise. This type of jointing is never as strong as a solid piece of wood, but it is strong enough for many purposes such as back rails for carcase work.

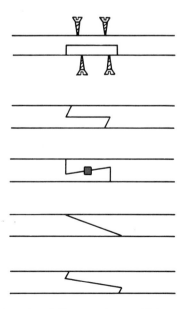

Lap-joint, and variations on the scarf joint

There are several variations, but the only reasonable ones for the home wood-worker are the lap-joint and the true scarf.

The lap is simply that – a lap. The two ends are marked and cut away so that each butts up to, and beds down to, the other. Adhesive and screws will bond them together.

The length of the lap should be at least one-and-half times the width of the material, and the cutting-away dimension should be half the thickness. These joints may be under-cut to give greater strength.

True scarf joints are tapered. Each piece is tapered (for one-and-a-half times the width) to a thin end. The two pieces are then glued and screwed to make one longer piece.

Cutting is by handsaw and finishing by the smoothing plane.

Joint variations

As your skill grows, more complex jointing may be attempted. Joints that have a value in enhancing appearance (or in hiding the unsightly) are in the main the same joints as before, but with minor modification.

Mitred mouldings

Where a frame is to hold a pane of glass or a panel (such as a window or door) the construction material will have either a groove and a moulded edge, or a rebate and a moulded edge. The problem is to marry the mouldings at each corner.

The technique for the rail (the tenoned member) would be to plane, mark out, make the tenon cheek cuts, plough the rebate, run the moulding and then cut the shoulders of the tenons. The procedure is the same whether you are running the moulding and rebate by hand or whether you are using an electric router.

Now that the rail and the stile have been shaped and made ready, all that remains is to marry the mouldings. Mitring is the simplest method. For this the two ends of the moulding are cut at 45°, so that when the frame is closed there will be no gap – simple a neat mitre line.

For this job you need a mitre template, which may be bought or made from pieces of beech. Two flat pieces, each about 150 × 56 × 10 mm (6 × 2¼ × ⅜ in), are glued and pinned together, and the resultant 'L' shape section has its ends cut at 45°.

Mitred mouldings

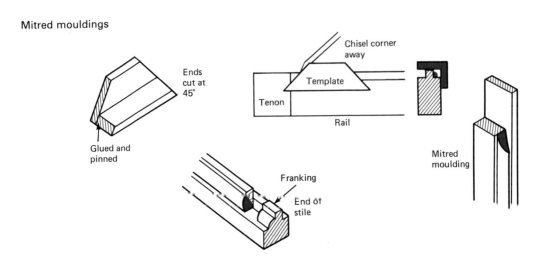

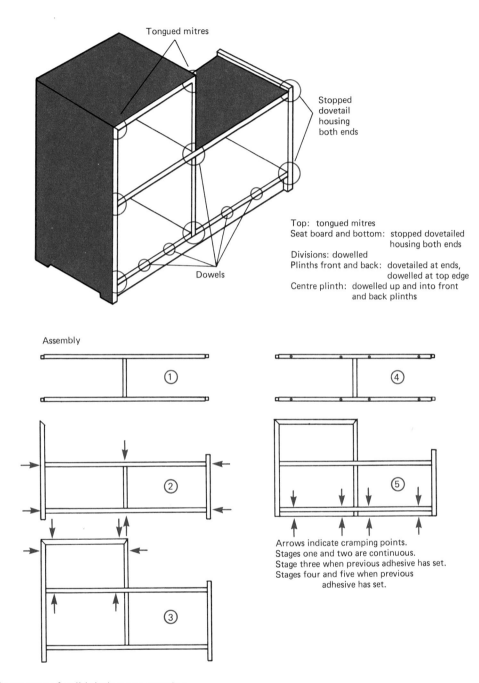

Tongued mitres

Stopped
dovetail
housing
both ends

Dowels

Top: tongued mitres
Seat board and bottom: stopped dovetailed
housing both ends
Divisions: dowelled
Plinths front and back: dovetailed at ends,
dowelled at top edge
Centre plinth: dowelled up and into front
and back plinths

Assembly

① ② ③ ④ ⑤

Arrows indicate cramping points.
Stages one and two are continuous.
Stage three when previous adhesive has set.
Stages four and five when previous
adhesive has set.

A telephone seat of solid timber construction

Scribed mouldings

Mitres look neat when close-fitting; but if the material shrinks, the mitre will open and look bad. A better method is to short-scribe. A scribe, in woodworking, is where one moulding fits over another; one is the precise reverse of the other. The final appearance is still that of a mitre; but if the material shrinks there will be no gap, for the male mitred member will simply pull slightly out from the other.

To start on this form of joint proceed as for the moulding mitre, but do not mitre

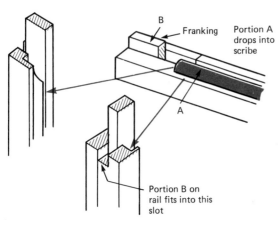

B
Franking
Portion A drops into scribe

A

Portion B on rail fits into this slot

Scribed moulding

the mould on the stile – the mortised piece. Mitre the rail moulding as before and then, using a curved outline presented by the mitre as it crosses the moulding, use a gouge (curved-edged chisel) to hollow out the moulding to fit the outline edge.

Use of joints

The front view of a telephone seat made from solid wood is shown on page 49. The construction would be very different if applied to chipboard. The joints are chosen for maximum strength, but they could be varied, especially if an electric hand router is available. The stopped dovetailed housings could become tongued housings, as could the division joints, which are shown as dowelled joints. With both constructions a back is essential to give rigidity. The back, of 6 mm (¼ in) ply, could be rebated in, glued and screwed. The main timber would need to be finished in a size not less than 18 mm (¾ in).

Chapter 6 Assembly methods

Assembly begins when all joints have been cut and fitted. It includes testing the assembly and cramping, final sanding of the inaccessible surfaces and edges, preparation of cramps, cramping methods and protecting packs and choice and preparation of adhesives. At this stage assembly proper can commence, with sub-assemblies (bases, drawers, pigeon hole divisions, etc.) being made up. The drawer units and bases could be left until the main carcase has been glued and is in cramp, thus saving time.

Sanding

Better-quality abrasive papers cost more but work more easily; these are garnet and aluminium oxide papers. Their abrasive grits are often coloured yellow, orange or green, so check with the supplier. Most sheet abrasive has a printed indication on the back stating G for garnet or AO for aluminium oxide. These two abrasives cut much faster and last much longer than the yellow quartz (sand) paper which, contrary to its name, is mainly glass.

There are several standard gradings given to coated abrasives (their correct name) and the table here shows the relationship between these arbitrary codes and the types of abrasives and the general terms – coarse, medium and fine.

Traditional glasspaper codes (home use range)
0 (0 paper) = garnet 4/0 (150 grit)
F2 (fine two) = garnet 2/0 (100 grit)
M2 (middle two) = garnet 1/2 (60 grit)
S2 (strong two) = garnet 1 (50 grit)

For home use the middle range of papers is suitable. For softwoods, made smooth by planing, use glasspaper M2 or garnet ½ (60 grit); this is best followed by 1 or 1½ glasspaper or garnet 2/0 or 3/0 (100–120 grit). This will leave a surface ready for painting.

If the work is not plane-finished too well, start with S2 glasspaper or garnet 1 (50). For a very smooth finish that is ready for a varnish or wax, finish with glasspaper 0 or garnet 4/0 (150). The grades for aluminium oxide are identical to those for garnet.

For flat surfaces use a cork rubbing block with the sheet paper torn into either four or six pieces. Place the paper on the block at an angle; the corners may then be turned up for gripping. As the paper clogs or wears, rotate it 90° and so on. This maximises use of the paper.

To divide the paper, tear it using a steel straight-edge (steel rule). With the rule pressed flat down against the paper backing, pull up from one corner towards the straight-edge and the paper will tear easily and cleanly.

Coated abrasives codes

Arbitrary Code	7/0	6/0	5/0	3/0	2/0	1/2	1	1½	
Grit screen size	240	220	180	120	100	60	50	40	and on
General terms		Extra fine		Fine		Medium		Coarse	

Found on the backs of abrasive sheets of garnet, aluminium oxide and silicon carbide.

Using the abrasive

Use firm strokes; the abrasive is supposed to cut – not polish. As far as is possible, keep to the line of the grain. As the edges of the wood piece are approached, lessen the pressure; rounded (dubbed) edges spoil a neat job, so keep corners sharp to look at.

Take the surface down stage by stage, for coarse paper will not give a final scratch-free surface even if it is worn out and you are using light strokes. It cannot be said too often that, when sanding, the work must be taken down by degrees. This applies also to electric orbital sanders, for no amount of abrasion by fine papers will flatten an unlevel surface.

Hardwoods and veneers scratch easily, so going down through the grades is even more essential. After the 150 grit garnet has been used it may be necessary to cut down even more to perhaps a 7/0 (240 grit), although this grade is really for de-nibbing lacquer finishes. For curly grains use finger touch and rotate the paper in small circular patches, only using straight strokes for the last few movements.

Order of sanding

Flat panels that may be reached easily after assembly should only be sanded down with the middle range of paper (60–100 grit) prior to assembly, for final sanding can be done later.

If flat panels are set in grooves, they must be sanded before assembly. Use a sheet of cardboard, free of wood chips, as a base and have a firm end stop. If a panel, or rail, moves while being sanded and there is no protection underneath, it will be scratched and dented.

All edges of rails that go between uprights, all inside leg faces, all mouldings – anything that will have a butted end when assembled – must be pre-sanded, for sanding blocks cannot cut close up into corners.

Cramping

Cramping entails the use of bar and sash cramps, G cramps, band cramps and edge cramps – all standard tools. With ingenuity, pressure may be applied with simple weights (even a bucket of water), wedges and lengths of string and, for small low-pressure jobs, rings cut from car inner tubes.

Whatever method of pressure is used, it is essential that the joints close well; for the thinner the adhesive-line, the greater the strength.

Always try joints together dry (without adhesive) and, if possible, cramp up the whole of the job; for any defective joint that needs adjustment will show up at this stage. The pre-cramping also enables you to decide on the method of cramping. Simple jobs do not need much thinking about. But where a job has several rails, one or two or more uprights, with a top and a bottom, pre-cramping is essential. Once the adhesive has been applied it is too late for you to find that you have no cramps. The best method for a complex structure is to do as they do in the furniture industry – break the job down into sub-assemblies, each of which is easier to handle than the complex whole.

There are several points to note when working out cramping schemes. Have you enough cramps? Are they large enough? Which part of the job must be glued first? Will later parts, or sub-assemblies, slide

Types of cramp, and methods of using them

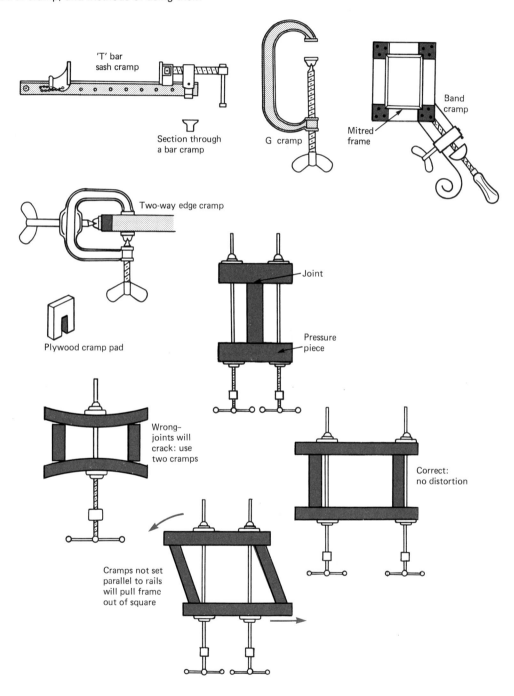

'T' bar sash cramp

Section through a bar cramp

G cramp

Mitred frame

Band cramp

Two-way edge cramp

Plywood cramp pad

Joint

Pressure piece

Wrong–joints will crack: use two cramps

Correct: no distortion

Cramps not set parallel to rails will pull frame out of square

Alternative cramping methods

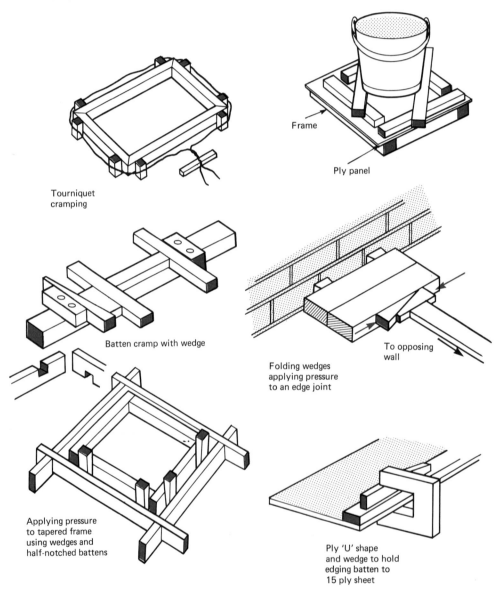

Tourniquet
cramping

Frame

Ply panel

Batten cramp with wedge

Folding wedges
applying pressure
to an edge joint

To opposing
wall

Applying pressure
to tapered frame
using wedges and
half-notched battens

Ply 'U' shape
and wedge to hold
edging batten to
15 ply sheet

on to their other halves? Will the cramps lay flat? Can the job be pulled square? Finally, are all joints pulling up? Do you need adjustment?

Squaring

Most jobs need to be square. However, very rarely do carcases come completely square. There is almost always at least one component that has a slight curvature, and a try square large enough to check from face to adjacent face will not register correctly. The method is to check from corner to corner, using a sharp-pointed, thin stick. These corner lengths give the diagonal lengths and each is marked for each direction. Continue to move the cramp position until the diagonals are of approximately equal length.

General rules for cramping are:
- Clean up inner edges of work.
- Assemble dry.
- Plan and arrange cramping system.
- Cramp dry.
- Check shoulders, flatness and squareness.
- Knock apart and adjust if necessary.
- Re-assemble, but leave joints as open as possible.
- Apply adhesive, especially to shoulders.
- Cramp up.
- Check diagonals with squaring stick and adjust cramps until diagonals of any rectangular area are equal.
- Insert glued wedges if any and drive them home, driving in each outer wedge first.
- Either wipe off surplus adhesive or wait for it to jell, then slice it away with a chisel.

Cramping problems

Shoulders open while under pressure:
   Tenon too long.
   Haunch too long.
   Tenon shoulders out of square.

Frame out of square:
   Tenon shoulders out of square.
   Haunch too long.
   Sash cramps not parallel to the edge of the rail.
Frame in winding – twisted:
   Cramps not flat on bench.
   Work not flat down in cramps.
Rails bowed:
   Too much pressure.
   Cramps incorrectly positioned.

Alternative cramping

If thin plywood is being glued to a made-up frame, pin it as well as gluing it or arrange a full bucket of water on battens to hold the joint area closed or use house bricks.

For smaller frames, use string and exert pressure by twisting as a tourniquet (Spanish windlass). Corners must be protected to avoid the string cutting into them; use folded, worn abrasive paper or smooth offcuts of wood. Wedges and folding wedges may be used to apply considerable pressure.

Simple batten cramps may be made using a length of old rafter or similar heavy batten and screwing on two end stops. Joints would then be closed by wedging.

For light frames, instead of screwing end blocks on to the main batten, drive two large screws partly home and then use these to create pressure by driving in a pair of wedges.

Yet another suggestion is to knock up

an all-enclosing frame from battens and then drive wedges down between the job and these battens to create pressure on the job.

Some of the temporary cramps mentioned, and also the application of folding wedges to apply pressure, are shown on page 54.

Complex jobs

Jobs such as chair frames and panelled carcase frames need breaking down into stages. If the job is a four-legged table, the two pairs of ends will be cramped first. The joints will be haunched mortise and tenon joints, with the ends of the tenons mitred if they are to meet (see the drawing).

To save cramping time, especially if only a single pair of cramps are available, glue, cramp, and then pin tenons, releasing them gently and standing them carefully aside. When two pairs have been made and the adhesive has set, clean out

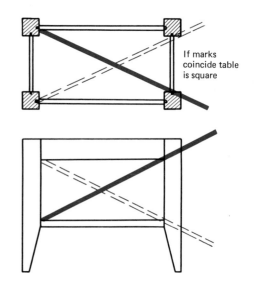

If marks coincide table is square

Squaring the table using a stick

the second set of mortises and finally cramp in the side rails. Fix with panel pins, making sure the pins are not near the leg face. Pin from the inside leg face, never from the outer face.

When the table frame has been completely glued and cramped, check all diagonals both from leg to leg and from rail to rail.

Adhesives

There are many adhesive types, but in practice there are only three – all synthetic – that have general application for wood constructions (jointing). The final environment of the job will determine the choice of adhesive. (Scotch glue, the traditional animal adhesive, is still used for veneering; but its use requires skill. It is rather messy and needs special preparation, so for home woodwork it is perhaps best left.)

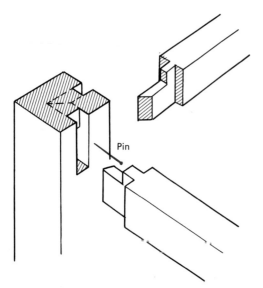

Pin

Haunched and mitred table-leg tenons

The end environment for most home-produced woodwork is in the home or in the garden. Within the home, some areas are damper than others (lofts or bathrooms) and need a damp proof adhesive. Garden furniture is subject to wet and damp conditions; living area furniture is subject to warm air and dry conditions; and bathrooms tend towards the warm and damp.

To suit these conditions there are urea formaldehyde adhesive, which is to all intents and purposes water-proof; casein adhesive, which is water-resistant but not to the extent of urea resins; and polyvinyl acetate, which is again water-resistant but to much less a degree than urea or casein.

Urea

For garden and garage work, windows and door frames and exterior doors, the most suitable adhesive is urea formaldehyde. This may be bought under several trade names and is made either as a white powder, to which water must be added, or as a clear syrup that requires contact with an acid catalyst (hardener) to set off (cure). The acid is painted over one member of the joint and the adhesive syrup over the other.

Once the two joint parts are brought together, chemical reaction begins and the adhesive begins to cure. The process cannot be reversed, so make sure all is in order before commencing.

With the powdered variety, the acid catalyst is already mixed with the resin adhesive; it requires only the addition of water for reaction to commence. Never put a damp stick or other damp tool into the tin of powder; there may be enough water on it to start the irreversible process of cure.

Most of the adhesive manufacturers that produce the powered variety instruct you to measure the water and add the powder to it, stirring as you go. This avoids lumps, but is not so simple as it sounds. How much water do you need? How fast should you add the powder? How much powder will the water take? These and other questions are unanswerable until you have wasted a lot of adhesive and time.

A good, simple and practical method of mixing adhesive powder and water (resin or casein) is to estimate the powder requirements (and you always need less than you think) and to put this amount into a plastic yoghurt container. Then drip in the water, drop by drop, mixing first as a dough, then as a stodgy thick paste and finally as a thickish, but free-flowing, cream. Stir rapidly until bubbles form on top and then leave the mixture to stand for 10–20 minutes. You can apply it immediately, but it will not be as creamy as it should be for easy spreading.

Paint a thin coat on both parts of the joint and clamp up.

Casein

The treatment for casein-based adhesives is the same as the treatment for ureas. Mix to a smooth cream, allow to stand, then apply and cramp.

PVA (polyvinyl acetate)

Probably the most popular all-purpose wood adhesive, this comes as a pure white creamy fluid, usually in squeezer applicators for small amounts. Larger quantities are pre-packed in large tins or plastic buckets.

Simply paint on a thin film to both members of the joint and cramp up.

Cramping times

Casein, at normal temperatures, is best left cramped for a minimum of four hours, when it will be ready to allow light work and movement. If heavy working is necessary on the cramped job immediately after release from the cramp, leave it in the cramp for longer – up to six hours.

Urea adhesives need about the same time as casein. The criteria are the room temperature and the load that the newly released job will have to carry. If no work has to be done immediately on release, four hours is ample; if further cramping of the assembly to other parts is needed, leave the first cramping for six hours. The warmer the room, the faster the adhesive sets.

PVA sets by evaporation of the solvent into the surrounding wood, so softwoods need less time in the cramp than hardwoods. Softwoods may be released for light handling in 20 minutes; but for further cramping and heavy work, one hour is best.

Cleaning

However careful you have been in the application of the adhesive, some is certain to squeeze out.

Casein may be washed off with a wet cloth; but do not over-wet the wood, for this raises the grain and means you will have to sand into difficult corners. Casein leaves a mild yellow stain at the joint if too much has been applied, so keep excess down to a minimum. Urea excess may be wiped away with a damp – not wet – cloth, but do not rub so hard that the adhesive is rubbed into the grain. PVA may also be wiped away with a damp cloth.

However, on the practical side, you are advised not to wipe any adhesive off, unless of course you have applied it too liberally; all adhesive will soak into the grain if it is wetted, and once there it will be impossible to remove. The most sound practical treatment is to allow the adhesive about 20 minutes to jell (that is, practically set) and then to use a very sharp bevel edge chisel to pare the jelly carefully away.

One final point about urea. If any ferrous metal (iron) comes into contact with the wet adhesive, blue stains will appear on the wood. So mix carefully in plastic containers, stir with a piece of dowel and protect cramping points with paper.

Final cleaning

When removing the assembly from the clamps, check all joints for excess adhesive. Chisel away any surplus adhesive and use a cabinet scraper to remove the glaze that such excess leaves. The glaze will show white through any stain or polish applied later.

Scrape away any slight imperfections that are seen on the external surfaces and then go through the whole sanding routine – coarse, medium, fine. Re-sand those internal edges that will be visible on the finished job, using the smooth paper. The job will be almost ready for final finishing once this is done.

One job that needs to be done at this stage is to check the standing level of any table, chair or stool. Stand the item on a flat surface and check to see whether it rocks. If so, use a fine tenon saw and take a slight cut from the bottom of one of the two legs on which it is rocking; cut and check – cut and check. When correct, sand the leg end smooth. Remember, only one leg will need to be cut.

Stopping

This is the name given to the process of filling any surface defects with wood filler (stopping). In the trade filling means grain filling (the process of filling the millions of cell cavities that soak up lacquer as it is applied), whereas stopping means filling surface defects. Thus the terms stopping and filling tend to be used for both jobs – that of filling holes, large or small.

The materials used for stopping blemishes vary. Wood polishers use wax, gum, resins, plasters and any material that suits their purpose, for the trade is highly skilled and the craftsmen are individualists. Joinery workers tend to use only those plaster-based materials that may be purchased ready-mixed, either with a water solvent or one of the polyurethanes. Both are of high quality, but the polyurethane base tends to have a higher water resistance than the other.

These stoppings may be purchased in almost any colour to match basic wood tones, so choose the best for the job. They go lighter in colour as they set, so choose slightly darker than would appear necessary.

Identify the defect, brush all dust away and use a thin knife or blade to force in, or scrape over, the stopper, until a slightly raised surface is left. Where nails and pins have been punched below the surface, as they should have been (if not, do it now), an air block may form below the stopper. Use the point of a sharp knife to squeeze in the stopping from one edge of the hole until there is a solid blob filling the hole.

Do not over-wet stopping; this thins it to the point of allowing it to flow into the grain and makes subsequent transparent finishing difficult. Use the stopping straight from the tin, place a curl of damp rag in the tin and replace the lid – tightly.

Leave the job to dry for as long as necessary (large holes take longer than small ones) and then sand off when the stopping will paper away easily to dust.

Re-fill any remaining defects. Brush away all dust and then, using the finest abrasive paper available, soften any sharp corners. This should not be done harshly, for the softening of the eges should only be noticeable to the touch, not to the eye.

Brush off and the job is ready for final surface finishing.

Chapter 7
Working drawings and marking out

It is easy to measure upwards from the floor, to make a mark on a wall, to drill and plug and to fix brackets. But if the shelf runs downwards and its back barely touches the wall, what have you achieved?

If the carefully made hi-fi unit starts to slide in easily but sticks halfway back because the fireside alcove runs narrow towards the back, again what have you achieved? And even more unnerving, if you have carefully brought home melamine teak panels all nicely parallel and straight and you then work in from the wall at each end and find, in the middle at the top, 75 mm (3 in) gap that has no reason to be there, what do you say to that?

So there is no choice. You must make preliminary drawings (which may be sketches) and from these you must either make further, and more detailed, drawings from which to work direct, marking the planed wood for each joint, or you must work by direct marking on to the wood and risk cutting incorrectly; once cut away, a line/length cannot be checked back to an original.

The time spent in planning, measuring and marking will be amply repaid by the saving in time during cutting, assembly and fixing – and the cost will be kept to a minimum. Remember no two deliveries of melamine board can be guaranteed to match in colour and a mis-cut board will ruin a half-completed job. In the same way, there are many shades of white.

Measuring

All wood constructions must fit into, on to or around something. So once you have settled on the idea, check the proposed final position.

Walls are rarely truly vertical, ceilings slope and corners are rarely truly square, whether they are internal (into the corner) or external (round a corner).

Central heating pipes, even radiators, sometimes infringe upon the planned site of the proposed cabinet. A simple thing like the return end of a window board is sufficient to stop the carefully planned writing desk from fitting, although these return ends rarely project more than the skirting at floor level. Bear in mind, too, that legs or a plinth set flush to the back will keep a simple bedside cabinet out from the wall although you wanted it flush. Even a small table for the hall requires positional planning to make sure the door does not bang into it each time it is opened. Skirtings will always need an allowance on planning. So measuring is vitally important.

Measuring is done with long folding rules, steel tapes or pinch rods. Pinch rods are two thin, lath-like sticks, each at least as long as three-quarters of the length (width) or height of any opening that you propose to measure. A plumb bob (lead weight) and line and a spirit level are also useful.

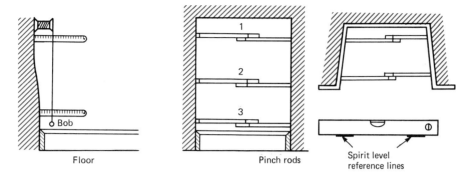

Floor · Pinch rods · Spirit level reference lines

Using a plumb bob, pinch rods and spirit level to measure a recess

Measuring recesses

Check the walls for plumb and straightness. Hold the line of the plumb bob high up the wall and watch the bob swing. As it settles, the line of the wall may be seen. It may be necessary to hold the top end away from the wall by using the end of a cotton reel; some walls are 50 mm (2 in) or more out of plumb. Make rough sketches, working on each wall and noting its direction of slope, if any. Check each of the three sides of the opening, noting any bad misalignment. For ceiling and floor levels, mark a horizontal line along the wall anywhere between floor and ceiling and measure up for the ceiling and down to the floor. Floors are usually sufficiently horizontal to work to; ceilings are not.

However, having said all this, please remember that such measurements are purely for general guidance, for no unit should be too tightly made. If true fitting is required, make the unit a nominal size that you know will fit and then scribe edgings along the top and down each side. Wall-to-wall cupboards are most often fitted in this manner.

Pinch rods are used by holding both sticks in one hand, pinched together. They are slid out and meet the sides (or floor to ceiling) of any opening you are measuring.

As they are gripped, with one end of each touching a wall, a pencil mark is made across them both. A new position (top and bottom) is checked and each time a pencil mark is made.

The difference between the maximum and minimum width of an opening is the difference between the longest spaced pairs of marks and the shortest. This is not the end of wall measuring however, for the difference in width of any opening may be at the top, bottom or in the middle. Or, as is most often the case, neither wall is vertical or straight.

Setting out

Having decided on the maximum sizes of any project, a working rod should be made. A working rod is a full-size drawing; it is called a rod because in the factory it is just that, the pertinent lengths of any jobs being marked on to a long, smooth board. For home working a long strip of wall paper will do, especially if its is pinned or taped down to a strip of hardboard about 300 mm (12 in) wide.

Rods should contain all the information for making the job. Imagine you are making a job for a retirement cottage a good few miles away; you cannot keep popping over to check measurements. Heights, widths, depths, timber cross-sections (width and thicknesses after planing),

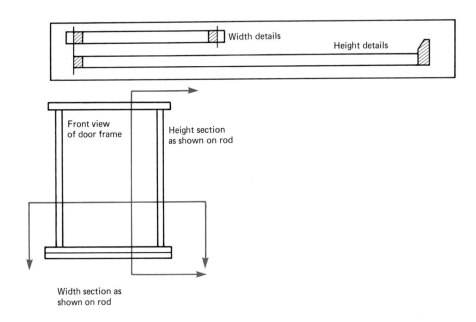

Height and width sections drawn on the rod board

Further details added to the rod, which now gives full information on the height and width sections

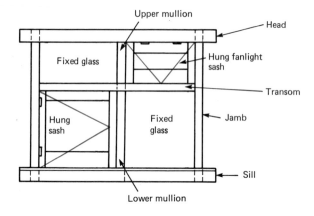

Front view of the garage window frame, showing the terminology used

shoulder lines for any tenoned rails, mortise lengths, widths and positions, glass sizes and rebate depths should all be on the rod.

If, for example, you are making a window frame for a garage, with perhaps four panes of glass, two of which are in hung sashes that open, the rod will be made as follows:

● Work always with the top of the job to your left and the face (the inner side of the frame) towards you.

● Use a try square to strike two lines across the board, whose distance apart will be the height/length of the finished frame.

● Measure from the line just struck on your left a distance equal to the horizontal width of the frame and strike across another line.

At this stage we have both height and width always available for reference when working.

Now work out how wide the planed timber sections for the various parts of the outer frame will be, and on the rod draw two parallel lines between height and width end lines. These lines will turn the heights and widths into rectangular sections.

From now on the rod must be thought of as being a series of cut sections, showing the true shape and position of any wood that would be revealed if you actually had a frame that was cut across vertically and horizontally.

The thickness of the top cross piece (of the frame), which is called the head, is marked across the height section. The thickness of the two side pieces (the jambs) is marked on the width section. The measurements of the lower horizontal piece (the sill) are marked on the height section at the extreme right.

At this stage you refer to your first pencil sketch of the front appearance of the frame and decide how high up you want the transom to be. The transom is the solid wood piece that runs from side to side and separates the top windows from the bottom. This height is purely a matter of choice, although mostly it is about one quarter of the total height down from the top.

The front view of the finished frame shows two sashes (opening windows) fitted into the frame, with the fixed windows having the glass directly glazed (fitted) into the frame itself. This is easily done and is cheaper in materials, but it does not look very good. It would be normal to make four sash frames and then to hinge two and fix two.

No written dimensions are given on the rod, for you will be working, later on, directly to the lines drawn by laying the timber on the rod. Before making the rod, check the exact sizes of materials that are available to be purchased.

The position of the transom is shown by drawing a rectangle giving the transom thickness on the height rod. The mullion (the vertical intermediate member between the sashes) is marked on the width section.

The sizes of the section will, as has been said, be that of the sizes available. But, as a guide for this type of work, the framing will be ex (out of rough sawn material before planing) 100 × 50 mm (4 × 2 in) and will finish 95 × 45 mm (3¾ × 1¾ in). The sashes will be of moulded stock sections with a finished size of 41 × 41 mm (1⅝ × 1⅝ in). The rebates for the sashes on this job will be formed by nailing on 'stop' strips which, while being less sound weatherwise, will save the laborious job of rebating at home.

To make the front appearance regular, the transom and the mullions will need to be thinner than the jambs and the head, and finish about 30 mm (1³⁄₁₆ in). The

Cutting list for four-light window (one-off)

Item	Name	No	Length	Sawn		Planed		Material
				Width	Thickness	Width	Thickness	
1	Jambs	2	1200 mm 4 ft	100 mm 4 in	50 mm 2 in	95 mm 3¾ in	45 mm 1¾ in	Planed softwood
2	Head	1	1125 mm 3 ft 9 in	100 mm 4 in	50 mm 2 in	95 mm 3¾ in	45 mm 1¾ in	Planed softwood
3	Sill	1	1125 mm 3 ft 9 in	150 mm 6 in	64 mm 2½ in	145 mm 5¾ in	59 mm 2⁵⁄₁₆ in	English oak or keruing
4	Transom	1	1125 mm 3 ft 9 in	100 mm 4 in	32 mm 1¼ in	95 mm 3¾ in	30 mm 1³⁄₁₆ in	Planed softwood
5	Top mullion	1	300 mm 12 in	100 mm 4 in	32 mm 1¼ in	95 mm 3¾ in	30 mm 1³⁄₁₆ in	Planed softwood
6	Bottom mullion	1	900 mm 3 ft	100 mm 4 in	32 mm 1¼ in	95 mm 3¾ in	30 mm 1³⁄₁₆ in	Planed softwood
7	Bottom sash stiles	4	900 mm 3 ft	45 mm 1¾ in	45 mm 1¾ in	Stock section size		
8	Top sash stiles	4	280 mm 11 in	45 mm 1¾ in	45 mm 1¾ in	Stock section size		
9	Sash top rails	4	500 mm 1 ft 8 in	45 mm 1¾ in	45 mm 1¾ in	Stock section size		
10	Sash bottom rails	4	500 mm 1 ft 8 in	64 mm 2½ in	45 mm 1¾ in	Stock section size		
11	Stop moulding	–	9 metres 30 ft	50 mm 2 in	13 mm ½ in	Stock section		Softwood
12	Transom weather strips	–	1200 mm 4 ft	25 mm 1 in	25 mm 1 in	Stock section		Softwood

meeting corners of the stops are mitred and cut in after the frame has been assembled.

For convenience, a full list is shown (see table) for a window that is a nominal 1200 ×1050 mm (4 ft × 3 ft 6 in). These dimensions should be modified to suit the run of brick courses for any particular wall (which is another reason for measuring). This adaption to existing work will save trouble in cutting bricks. In practice the cutting list is made from the finished rod.

All dimensions on the list can only be approximate, for the precise outer dimensions of the actual job will control them.

No finished lengths are shown on any cutting list, for these lengths are struck off the rod on to the planed timber. Where stock sections are bought, only nominal sawn sizes are given. This helps you and the retailer choose.

Sections

Once the rectangular outlines of the planed framing have been drawn in, their shapes are put in. Because the rebates are to be formed by planted stops, all of

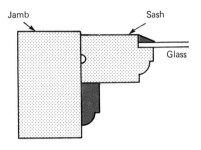

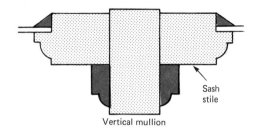

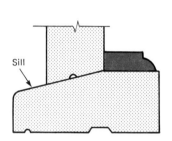

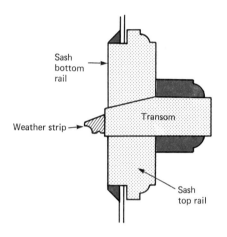

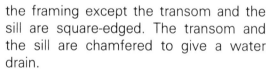

Sections through the entire window frame

the framing except the transom and the sill are square-edged. The transom and the sill are chamfered to give a water drain.

The sash material needs to be shown now before the joint details are added (see diagram). The sash stock sections and the sill section should be checked against the standard sections available.

Joints

Sash joints are mortised and tenoned with the moulding mitred and the outside edge of the material 'franked' as shown on page 50. Draw in the tenons and mortises to the proportions described on page 33. Indicate the rail shoulder lines, then draw in the mortise positions on the frame material and indicate the shoulder lines.

You will notice that all shoulders are square across except for the tenons on the lower ends of the upper and lower mullions and the tenons on the lower ends of the jambs (see drawing). As the transom and the sill are weathered (i.e. sloped), the outer shoulders of all of the tenons of vertical members must be sloped. This is called scribing.

Other rods

The rod for the specified window frame is now complete. Other jobs may need more sections, horizontal or vertical, for a door may have panels below the middle rail or lock rail, or the job may be a hi-fi unit with shelves at the ends and cupboard storage in the middle. This would need at

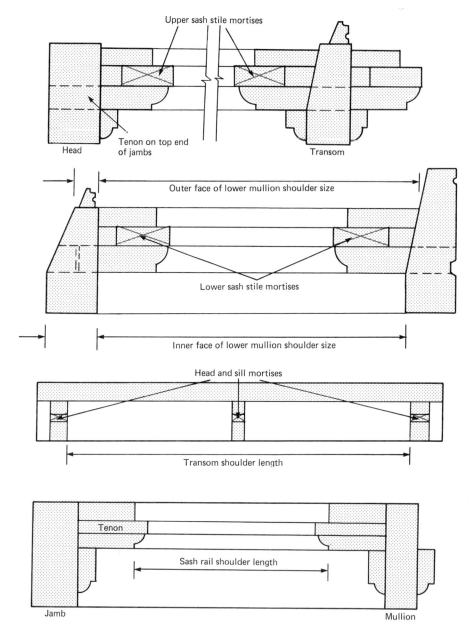

Upper sash stile mortises

Tenon on top end
of jambs

Head

Transom

Outer face of lower mullion shoulder size

Lower sash stile mortises

Inner face of lower mullion shoulder size

Head and sill mortises

Transom shoulder length

Tenon

Sash rail shoulder length

Jamb

Mullion

Sections through the entire window frame

least two end sections – one through each part. For the same unit possibly three width sections may be needed – one through the top layer, one through the centre and one through the plinth base.

However, all this sounds complex and, indeed, some rods are. But the saving in time and aggravation that a rod achieves

makes the job worth while. All shaped panels may be shown if the paper is wide enough. Slot and hole positions may be clearly located and any shaped moulding sections may be shown.

A simple example to show the value of the rod form of approach is to visualise again the hi-fi unit mentioned. It will obviously have a top, a lower top and a bottom. But the top may be planned to over-run the ends, so how much longer is it than the bottom and lower top that fit between the sides? The middle ends or vertical divisions run from the upper face of the bottom to the lower face of the lower top. The top divisions run from the lower face of the true top down to the upper face of the lower top. A few pencil lines show this accurately; if you try to calculate, somewhere you will go wrong – we all do. In practice, for such a job the rod sections would be marked out on the melamine board, but you must have a clear picture of your planned job before buying or cutting.

Drawings for a hi-fi unit

Cutting lists

Once the rod is made, the materials list is made. Lay on the rule, measure the largest item first for length, width and thickness, working on one rod section for widths and thickness and the other rod section for the lengths.

On the frame rod measure the length of the jambs, allowing approximately 25 mm (1 in) for waste. Then measure the jamb width and thickness. Record all this. Then measure the transom and so on.

When the cutting list is complete obtain the materials and, if necessary, saw and plane them to size.

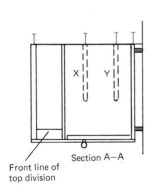

Section A–A

Front line of top division

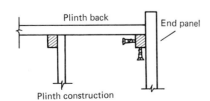

Plinth construction

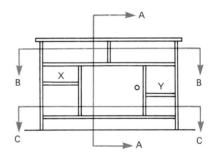

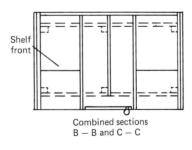

Combined sections B – B and C – C

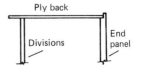

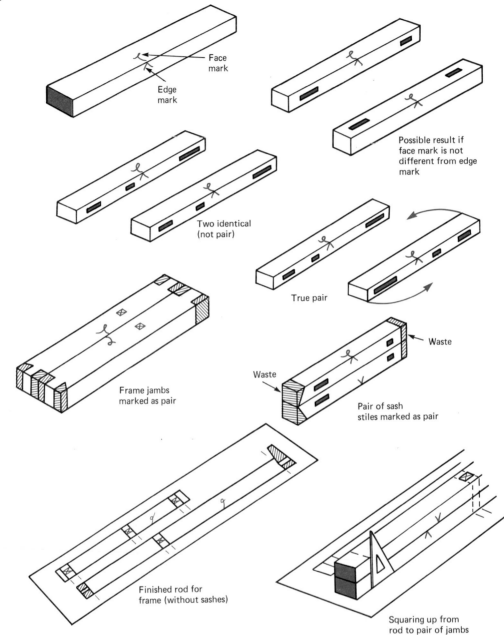

Face mark

Edge mark

Possible result if face mark is not different from edge mark

Two identical (not pair)

True pair

Waste

Waste

Frame jambs marked as pair

Pair of sash stiles marked as pair

Finished rod for frame (without sashes)

Squaring up from rod to pair of jambs

Marking out the window-frame components

Marking out

Study each piece of wood (for any job) and select the best face and edge to show. Mark these by using a very clear, hooked line on the face and a 'V' sign on the face edge. The two pieces for the jambs must be paired, as must all eight of the sash stiles (see diagram).

Start marking the joints by laying the pair of jambs on the rod and then square up from the shoulder lines across the edges of the jambs. Square up the mortise lines for the transom mortise. Now turn each piece over until the face side is uppermost and then square the lines across the face. The lower end of each jamb will have two shoulder lines squared across because of the bevel to fit the sill.

Set the mortise gauge to the chisel you are going to use to chop out the mortise and mark, from the face edge, both the top and bottom tenons and the mortise for the transom.

Square the sets of lines right round, marking all faces, and gauge the tenons and mortises on the back of the job, again working from the face edge with the gauge.

For a job of this size the mortises should be no narrower than 18 mm (¾ in) and will be positioned about 28 mm (1⅛ in) in from the face edges of the material, not centrally. The jamb marking details are shown in the diagram. Once the mortises are marked, the bevelled shoulder can be put in. The jamb marking is then complete.

The head and the sill are marked for their mortises by laying them on the width rod and squaring up across their faces. The mortises are marked on both back and front faces, because the only sound way to cut mortises is to approach them from both sides.

Transom

This has square shoulders at both ends and is marked up from the width rod; the central mortise position is marked at the same time. The front edge of the transom is pencil-hatched to indicate where you will be planing off the bevel for the rain slope. This bevel is planed with the jack or smoothing plane after the tenons and the mortise have been cut.

The angle of the bevel should be checked with a sliding bevel, for the bevel on the sill and the bevel on the transom must be the same.

Mullions

There are two mullions: a short one, which is tenoned into both head and transom, and a longer one, which is tenoned into the transom and the sill.

The top ends of both of these have square-shouldered tenons, whereas the lower ends have scribed tenons. Scribing means that the tenon shoulder is cut to such a shape as to enable it to fit closely to any shape formed on the mortised member.

When previously marking the jamb lower ends, a bevel should have been set and kept set, for the lower ends of both mullions and both jambs are identical.

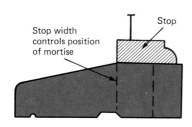

Marking out details for the jamb

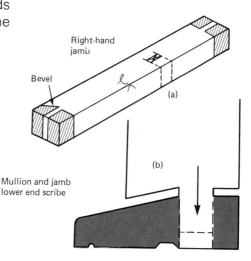

Mullion and jamb lower end scribe

More complex marking

In general all proposed cutting should be marked out on the job before any cutting commences. In this way the full picture is more easily kept in mind. Marking each stage and then cutting it separates activities in the mind. Only when the rod has been fully marked and the work fully marked from it, can the whole of your attention be given to the accuracy of cutting. If the mind wanders to other things so can the cutting tool. So all shapes, grooves, rebates and bevels should be marked before any cutting begins.

Rebates

Use a marking gauge, working from the face side and face edge of the work, to define the rebate for depth and distance on. Then cross-hatch the waste area with a pencil.

Grooves

Mark these exactly as you have the rebates. But, if possible, use a mortise gauge (twin spur) set to the width of the grooving tool cutting iron. Cross-hatch all waste.

Bevels

Bevels, in general, run from one edge fully across the edge of the work piece to the other edge – a full slope, in effect. Chamfers are bevels that do not run the full width of the face.

Bevels are marked by pencil along one face only, for they are finished with the smoothing plane and worked by eye until there is a straight flat slope from the high corner down to the pencil line. If the angle is critical, then mark both ends of the wood using a sliding bevel as a guide.

Chamfers are marked by two pencil lines, one on each adjacent face. If required, their ends may also be marked. Chamfers are again planed by eye.

The reason for pencil marking is that the points of gauges cut into the wood face at right-angles. If two such sharp cut lines are incised into the work, the bevel will have to be cut deeper than is required to remove these marks.

Pairs

One final word on marking. Remember that your hands are in pairs, palms up, thumbs out. There you have the marking for all the work that has two rails, etc at opposite edges of the job. When marked they must be seen both with their face sides up and both with their thumbs (face marks) pointing out. Then you have a pair. If the job is a door with a wider bottom rail than top rail, the stiles will have the two short mortises at the top and the long ones at the bottom. Without pairing at marking, this result may not be achieved.

Chapter 8
Surface finishing

After the job has been made and cleaned up, surface protection must be applied. This protection must satisfy three requirements. It must give the appearance you want; it must compatible with the wood used to enable it to give the appearance you want and it must be sufficiently durable to maintain the required appearance.

Not all finishes can be applied to all woods and not all finishes give equal durability.

Before any surface finish is applied, however, you must clean up the work thoroughly.

Cleaning up

All excess adhesive must be removed with the edge of a fine knife or chisel. Where too much water has been used to

Using and sharpening a cabinet scraper

wipe away adhesive during assembly, the adhesive will have flowed into the grain and this will prevent even absorbtion of stain. Adhesive in the grain will show up as a white glaze under all finishes other than paint.

Chisel carefully and do not cut into the wood. Then up-end the chisel (or knife) and scrape with the edge square to the wood. Finish with medium and fine abrasive paper.

Any joint not previously levelled must be smoothed flat with a sharp smoothing plane, or cabinet scraper, and finished with abrasive paper used on a cork block. The cabinet scraper is a flat silver-steel plate approximately 125 × 60 mm (5 × 2½ in) and very thin and flexible. It is made sharp by rubbing its edges square along a block-sharpening stone and then turning these edges over to give a hooked edge. You could call it a burr edge; but it is not, for a burr is rough. The scraper should have a fine, sharp edge angled to the main plate.

Where cramp pressure pads have marked the work, dampen the bruised area with hot water. Then cover it with a wet, thick cloth and press down with a hot iron. This turns the water into steam and drives it into the wood grain, which swells

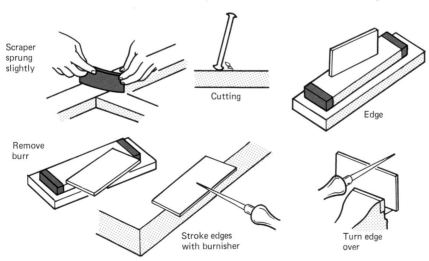

Scraper sprung slightly — Cutting — Edge — Remove burr — Stroke edges with burnisher — Turn edge over

and pushes out the dent. When dry, scrape and sand smooth.

Give the job a good brushing, then you can start finishing.

Softwoods may be painted, but harwoods hardly ever since they almost always have an appearance that may be enhanced by clear or semi-clear finishes. Softwoods in some designs may also present an attractive appearance under clear lacquer.

Creosote

For basic protection where there is likely to be a lot of exposure, creosote is a useful finish. It ranges from dark brown through to golden yellow. It has the effect of a preservative, filling the wood cells and killing the spore of fungi. It is applied to softwood and hardwood by liberal brush-coating or, on wood to be buried in the ground, by soaking.

Preservatives for a similar purpose may be bought in either a clear green or yellow finish. These are metallic and salt-based.

Paint

Painting is the most common method of weather protection, for paint has the additional characteristic of giving a decorative finish to the rather neutral softwoods on which it is used.

Paints are many and varied, so be advised by the retailer as to the best paint for the purpose. Generally the paints with the higher gloss are the most durable; many of the flat and eggshell finishes are suitable only for indoor work.

Mostly paint is brushed on, although the modern roller will apply it quickly to large areas. The surface must be prepared. Assuming you have new wood,

start from the carefully smoothed surface and apply knotting to all knots. Knotting is a shellac mix not soluble in turpentine. By painting knotting over all knots, the natural wood resins and oils are prevented from creeping through and spoiling the top paint finish.

Primer is applied over the knotting, when dry. This fills and seals the wood pores and prevents the wood from absorbing the paint solvents. It also offers a good base key for the paint. Two thin priming coats are better than one thick one. For interior work it is possible to achieve a good finish by using a thin coat of water-based emulsion paint as a primer.

When dry, and if rough, a light papering will improve the finished surface.

Following priming comes filling and stopping. Stopping is the process of filling holes and blemishes with either putty or plaster, or one of the proprietary wood stoppers. Cellulose or polyurethane stoppings are best for external work. The stoppings are knifed in and left to harden. Then they are sanded flat, dusted and given a dab of primer.

You may decide to fill in the minor grain ripples, although this is only necessary if you want the final paint surface to be mirror-like. A proprietary filler is rubbed well into and across the wood grain, using a coarse rag, and wiped off before the material sets. Again, light sanding is advisable after filling.

Now comes the undercoating. The undercoat used must have two main properties. It must flat out as it dries and it must obliterate colour variation in the base wood. Undercoats have a high pigment content and are thus much better than emulsion paint, which is often used by builders for a quick job. After drying, a light finger-touch sanding is given, followed by a good brushing.

Top coat

Modern gloss and semi-gloss paints require very little brushing out. They are laid on over as large an area as possible, subject to keeping the edge of the film wet-on-wet. Cross lightly at right-angles with an empty brush and lay off with very light strokes along the grain. Over-brushing will spoil modern paints as the resins used flash-off quickly and resist further brushing.

Two thin coats are better than one thick coat, especially if you time the application correctly. The first coat should be touch-dry or more, but not left so long that it has acquired a dust coat.

Order of work

Start at the top and work down. Panels in frames are painted first, then horizontal rails, then intermediate vertical members and finally outer vertical members. A fairly quick way to paint flush doors or other large flat areas is to apply the paint with a roller and then lay it off with a soft, wide paint brush.

New hardboard should be sealed with emulsion paint before it is painted with gloss.

At all times work fast enough to apply wet-on-wet to avoid lap-over showing on the final finish.

The various stages of stopping, filling and painting are shown in the diagram.

Enamels

Enamels are high-bodied (full of solids) and are usually made in very hard colours.

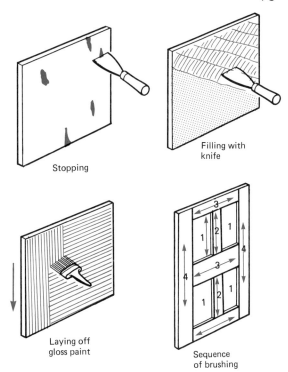

Stopping

Filling with knife

Laying off gloss paint

Sequence of brushing

Order of work for painting a door

They are applied by brush using a slightly different technique to that used with paints. Dip the brush into the enamel and make sure it is well loaded. The enamel should be flowed on rather than brushed on and should be brushed out less than paint; a thin-edged brush is best.

Lacquer finishes

Lacquer was the name given to early varnishes; but today lacquer has a rather specialist meaning, indicating that the surface finish referred to is a clear, colourless and hard gloss. The three most popular lacquers are polyurethane, cellulose and acid catalyst. This last is sold as two-part AC lacquer, which means that the base resin that forms the final coat is mixed with a retarding agent, which holds off the

74

set of the mixture. When the second part of the combination – the hardener – makes contact, the retarding agent is neutralised and the hardener acts as a chemical catalyst causing the lacquer to set.

Polyurethane

This gives a hard clear finish. It is tough, water and knock-resistant and it is not easily damaged by spirits or heat. Polyurethane may be bought as a transparent coloured coating in many bright colours, allowing the wood grain to show through.

Polyurethanes are supplied directly to the sanded wood surface by brush. Apply a full-flow coat and do not brush out too vigorously. Should the wood being coated be one that has a coarse, open grain, it is best to pre-fill with a polyurethane filler. Any stain used beneath polyurethane should be either water or naphtha stain, or one sold as compatible with PU lacquers.

Two-part PU lacquers are harder and tougher than the single pack variety; the two parts should be mixed together to the instruction of the maker. Brush across the grain and lay-off with a light touch along the grain.

When the final coat is dry, lightly sand the surface with a special rubbing-down abrasive paper that has a grit of silicon carbide. Final finishing is done with a hard furniture wax; use a little wax and rub in well. This produces an acceptable low-gloss finish. Polyurethane gloss from the brush is highly reflective and is an acquired taste.

The material sold as yacht varnish is mainly two-part PU and this should alway be the one used out-of-doors.

Cellulose

This is commercial spray finish material and is not easily brushed on because of its quick-setting characteristics. The solvent used will penetrate many other finishes. So if cellulose is brushed or sprayed on, test the undercoat first, otherwise reaction may take place.

Acid catalyst lacquer

This lacquer is very hard, very transparent and very glossy, although it may be matted down with wire wool and wax.

It comes as two parts, the lacquer and the hardener (catalyst). These are mixed to instruction and painted on. The acid catalyst will react with most other surface finishes, so always test first on a small area. During the hardening process vapour is released; this is toxic, so work in a ventilated area.

On exposure to weather AC sometimes goes cloudy, so use it for interior furniture.

Coloured lacquers

There are finishes on the market that consist of coloured polyurethane lacquer. Using these, it is possible to paint on colour and lacquer in one operation. The colours are not high-bodied, so the natural wood grain will show through. For regularly toned wood these give good results. But to achieve a colour match on wood of irregular colouring requires long practice; so for one-off jobs traditional staining has perhaps greater appeal.

Chapter 9 Practical projects

The following items of woodworking are included here for three reasons. They are examples of the application of basic woodworking to simple items that can be produced with basic tools. They include most of the processes previously described and show the manner in which these processes can be applied. They are also representative of the range of work a home woodworker may wish to begin with. They may all be modified to allow for variations in design or materials. All the projects need planning, measurement, working drawings, cutting lists and the use of tools and appropriate finishes.

The first project is presented in detail with full working instructions, which are intended to be representative of all woodworking activities. The later projects are given in outline only, each forming a basis for modification as required.

Hi-fi unit

The unit is a modern long and low version. The length must accommodate the units and sound equipment you have; the height will need to suit both the equipment and the record size; the front-to-back measurement must also accommodate the base of the main unit. Having said this, the project may be designed to suit individual taste. The drawings shown below will help you produce an individual cabinet, but check all sizes before obtaining any material.

Materials

Use teak finish (real wood veneers on chipboard) or teak-finished melamine surface boards, bought ready edged. The construction is the same for both boards, although the real wood veneers need final surface finishing in wax or teak oil and also edging with self-adhesive, real teak veneer edgings. The melamine panels need no surface finish and are ready edged (unless they are cut); ends must be melamine-edged wherever they show.

Construction

There are no joints or jointing procedures with hand tools in this project. The only hand tool work consists of accurate marking, scribing and sawing; hole-boring and rebating of back edges; and fitting of doors and edge veneering. All joints are assembled with knock-down (KD) fittings.

Think about the job, where it must go and the equipment it will have to contain. Then make a sketch and mark in approximate sizes. The back hardboard may now be purchased and used as a rod board so the cutting sizes of all materials may be worked out.

Lay the hardboard flat and tape on a reasonably smooth sheet of wallpaper – reverse side up. Mark on this a rectangle equal to the overall height and depth (end view). This marking is easy if the hardboard has square ends and parallel edges. Use a long thin strip of wood and cut a 'V' notch in one end. Working from the front edge, fit the pencil into the 'V' and, with the left hand gripping the stick, slide along the front edge of the board to mark two lines indicating the full depth. The height and floor lines are marked across the board.

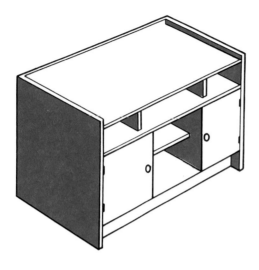

Hi-fi unit

Overall dimensions

Length 1220 mm (4 ft)
Height 610 mm (2 ft)
Depth 430 mm (1 ft 5 in)

Tools

Working bench top
Rule
Square
Panel saw
Plane
Hand drill
4.8 mm (³/₁₆ in) and 2.4 mm (³/₃₂ in) Morse drills
Bradawl
Hammer
Screwdriver
Craft knife
Electric iron
Cork sanding block
Gauge
Urea adhesive
Brown shoe-polish
Rag

Fittings

8 KD two-block fittings
2 pr lay-on rebated hinges
2 door knobs
2 magnetic catches
4 shelf supports
610 mm (2 ft) of 6 mm dowel
4 flush screw-cover buttons
Screws for above fittings
1 doz 32 mm (1¼ in) No 8 steel woodscrews
1 doz 12 mm (½ in) No 4 steel woodscrews
2½ doz 19 mm (¾ in) No 6 steel woodscrews
4 38 mm (1½ in) No 8 steel woodscrews
4 domes of silence (or castors)
1220 mm (4 ft) plastic back channel

Note: All screws may be standard bright mild steel woodscrews, but full threaded chipboard screws are more
secure.

Wood material

1 top
1 lower top
1 bottom
2 ends
2 doors
2 plinths
1 cross plinth
2 top divisions
2 lower divisions
1 shelf

All of 15 mm thick standard
450 mm boards of
melamine-faced chipboard

1 back, of 4 mm hardboard
3.7 metres (12 ft) 19 × 19 mm (¾ × ¾ in) planed
softwood
2 metres (6 ft 6 in) teak-finish iron-on edging

Judge and draw in the distance down from the end top edge to the top panel; make it about 25 mm (1 in). Draw in the thickness of the top – 15 mm (⅝ in). Draw in where the bottom will be – 15 mm (⅝ in) thick and about 50 mm (2 in) up from the floor line. Decide how high the doors are to be and draw in the lower top position. The centre shelf, if included, must also be drawn in.

Inside the back line draw a line to indicate the hardboard back thickness – 4 mm. Draw in the ends of the front and back plinths, but remember to check the size of the wall skirting if the unit is to go right back to the wall. Draw in this size and then mark the cut-out size at the lower back edges of the end panels. If the skirting is higher than the bottom panel,

you will have an unsightly gap inside the cabinet and a blocking strip will be needed. The front plinth is set back about 35 mm (1½ in) for toe room. The back rim sits on the top panel; the top edge of the back panel is screwed to it. You now have all the heights and widths.

The upright divisions will be screwed from below, while their top edges will be held by dowels. Before assembly, all meeting edges should be coated with a thin layer of adhesive and the surfaces that butt on to these edges must be deeply scored through the melamine face.

With melamine-edged boards it is not practical to take off the edging, fit the panels to each other and then re-apply the edging. So the procedure for hand work is always to arrange adjoining panels to

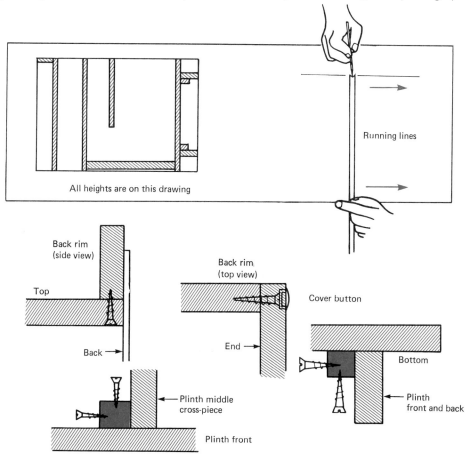

All heights are on this drawing

Running lines

Back rim (side view)

Top

Back →

Plinth middle cross-piece

Plinth front

Back rim (top view)

End →

Cover button

Bottom

Plinth front and back

Setting-out and construction of the hi-fi unit

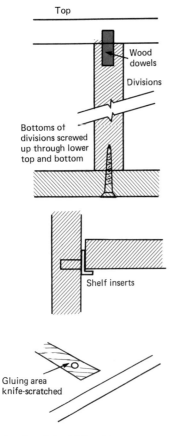

Further details of the hi-fi unit

show a definite break-line; this way it looks intentional. Any attempt to secure absolutely flush fitting is doomed to failure, for only machine-cutting and process assembly will achieve this. The doors in this unit fit between the lower top panel and the bottom panel, but inside the end panel and overlapping the division front edge. This gives a good appearance and makes life easier when cutting the doors to size.

Plan view

Having studied the end view on the rod and grasped the principle of the design, set out on the rod a plan view of the overall size. Judge and show the end views of all members that run front to back. These will be the end panels, the lower and upper divisions, the plinth centre crosspiece, the back and the shelf (giving the shelf width).

Allowing for setting back the divisions and shelves, as previously mentioned,

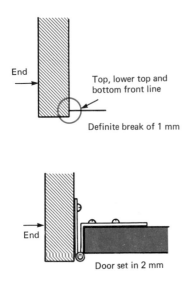

Door details for the hi-fi unit

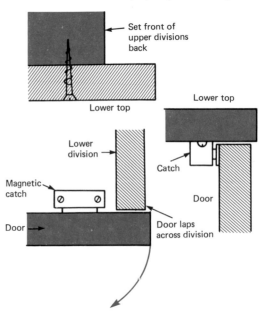

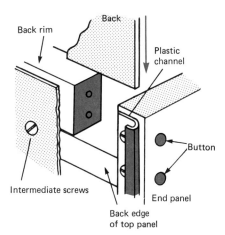

Back rim
Back
Plastic channel
Button
Intermediate screws
End panel
Back edge of top panel

Back detail for the hi-fi unit

make a full cutting list. The back is held in place by two vertical plastic channels and by intermediate screwing to the top, lower top, bottom and divisions.

The work

Check the cutting list and make sketched outlines of all panels and pieces on a scrap sheet of paper. Fit these into the standard size of the type of board you buy. The main panels will be out of two 2440 mm (8 ft) sheets and the other pieces should

Two 2440 x 457 mm (8 ft x $1\frac{1}{8}$ ft) and two 1832 x 457 mm (6 ft x $1\frac{1}{2}$ ft) boards

Top	Lower top

| Bottom | Plinth back |
| | Door | Door |

Back rim	Lower division
Plinth front	
Plinth cross rail	
Shelf	Upper division
	Upper division

| End | End | Lower division |

Board layout for the hi-fi unit

fit into two 1830 mm (6 ft) sheets. The design may have to be modified slightly to allow for the job to be fitted into standard size boards, for saw cuts must be allowed for. As an example, two 610 mm (2 ft) long ends and one 1220 mm (4 ft) long panel could not be cut from one 2440 mm (8 ft) board.

Having worked out the number of boards and their sizes, the immediate job is to check the finished lengths of each panel and then to cut off each panel size, allowing a slight over-length for planing. If each saw cut is scored across and all round each board, you are more likely to set chip-free edges. Pad the vice cheeks and plane each sawn end square. Now saw each piece to width, checking with the working rod each time.

Plane the sawn edges smooth and check for squareness. Identify those edges that need veneering and iron on the edge veneers. This is done using an iron set just hot enough to melt the adhesive. Try it out on a test piece; if the temperature is about right, the edging will pull off for about 50 mm (2 in) and then break. If the temperature is too low, the edging will not be tacky; if it is too high, the edging will peel right off leaving a sticky edge to the panel.

Starting from one end, guide the edge veneer by hand and press firmly with the hot iron. Immediately the length has been fully edged, press the edging firmly down with the side of a hammer handle. Check visually, and re-heat and press any uplifted areas. Trim the edge veneer with a sharp chisel or the edge of a cabinet scraper, then sand off at an angle to give a smooth finish. Only the end panel top edges and the door top edges should need edging.

When each panel is correctly sized and edged, mark them out for the KD fittings. Only the two ends and the top and lower top will have these – two to each butted

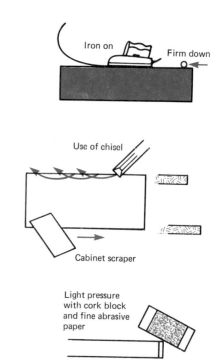

Ironing-on and trimming the edging

joint. The bottom panel will have a strip of the 19 mm (¾ in) square material glued and screwed down flush to each end, with the strip being left the exact length of the plinth centre cross rail. The two edges of the plinth front and back will have two pieces to each edge, leaving room for the centre cross rail.

KD fittings

The two-block fittings need careful positioning. Close the two parts together and visualise the action of the centre bolt; it must pull the two panels together. Separate the two parts and then screw, with a dab of adhesive underneath, the two parts of the blocks that do not have a centre nut, down on to the ends of the top and lower top panels. Set each block back by about 1 mm more to allow for tight pulling. The block positions across the boards are not critical; make a gauge of scrap wood so that all blocks will be tidily arranged the same amount in from the panel edges.

Now slip on the second parts of the blocks (the pieces with the inserted nuts) and offer each panel in turn to the correct end panel, marking the block outlines with a sharp scribe. Glue and screw the remaining four blocks on to the end panels.

Lay one end panel down flat (KD blocks up) and drop in both the top and lower top panels. Drop on the second end panel and screw up and support the lower end of the topmost end panel. Feed in the bottom panel and screw it home.

Set the cabinet on its feet and position the divisions until they are a smooth sliding fit. Mark along each side of the top and bottom edges of the four vertical divisions

in their correct positions. Dismantle the cabinet and, with a craft knife, score along the butting areas of all panels.

With a 6 mm (¼ in) drill, make holes centrally along the positions marked for the vertical divisions, but only on the undersides of the top and lower top. Make holes about 12 mm (½ in) deep. Carefully mark the division top ends to match and glue in eight short dowels (two to each edge). With a 3 mm (⅛ in) drill, drill down completely through the lower top panel and the bottom panel central to the marked butting areas for the divisions. Countersink the underside of the lower top panel holes. Assemble the plinth to the lower panel, screwing them together.

Smear adhesive on to the ends of the two top panels and on to the ends of the two divisions. Assemble the top panels with the two divisions and screw up into

Final assembly of the hi-fi unit

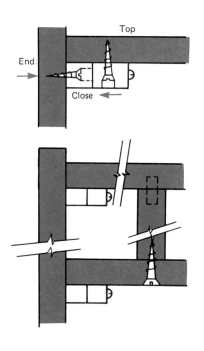

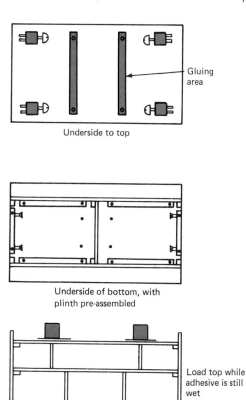

Underside to top

Gluing area

Underside of bottom, with plinth pre-assembled

Load top while adhesive is still wet

the lower ends of the divisions. Assemble the top unit and tighten the four KD bolts. If cramps are available, cramp over the top panel and the lower top to squeeze the top ends of the divisions up to the underside of the top panel. If no cramps are available, apply pressure later but work fast.

Turn the whole cabinet on to its top ends (on paper or cloth to prevent scratching); glue and drop in the two dowelled ends of the lower divisions. Glue both bottom ends of these divisions and also the ends of the bottom panel (which should already have the plinth glued and screwed to it). Slide in the bottom panel until it rests on the divisions. Check all alignments and screw the bottom into the ends; also screw up into the divisions.

Lay the cabinet on its front and either fix the back or pin on two diagonal laths to keep it square. Stand the cabinet on its lower edges and, again protecting the surface, put weights on the two top divisions. Wipe away excess adhesive with a damp cloth. Leave until all the adhesive has set – about four hours.

Final fitting

Fit the back rim by screwing from the ends and top panel. Fit the back grooved sections. Also fit the back panel by sliding it downwards and screwing into the top, bottom and division back edges. Mark and drill holes for the shelf fittings and fit the shelf.

Fit the doors, checking they have good clearance top and bottom and that they over-reach the division edges by 1 mm. Position the door hinges and attach them with one screw each. Hang the doors and test that they close all right. Make any adjustments, then put in the remaining screws. Fit the magnetic catches and door knobs.

Final cleaning

Wipe clean the finished job with a damp cloth. Rub any chipped edges with dark brown shoe polish and apply furniture cream to the whole unit to remove any finger marks.

Tiled table

Ceramic tiles may be laid in many arrangements on 18 mm (¾ in) chipboard to form a long or square table top. The adhesive used is tile cement, followed by grouting filler. The edges are protected by mitred hardwood strips of the same (or contrasting) hardwood as the base frame and legs.

If the table is square, then the lower rails could be diagonal (corner to corner); if rectangular, then an H-frame could be used. If the final design is long and low, then the underframe could be of round-edged slats to make a shelf. These would be tenoned into the lower side rails. Look at the suggestions in the drawing before you decide.

The work stages are as follows. Draw a sketch plan and finalise the size. Choose the tiles and arrange these to give the size of top panel required. Make a rod of the plan view of the table, showing all rails and the ends of the legs. Use the top panel for this rod. Turn the table top over and use the bottom side (or use a sheet of paper) to make a rod of the side elevation showing the height and leg positions (see diagram). Make a cutting list and obtain the timber.

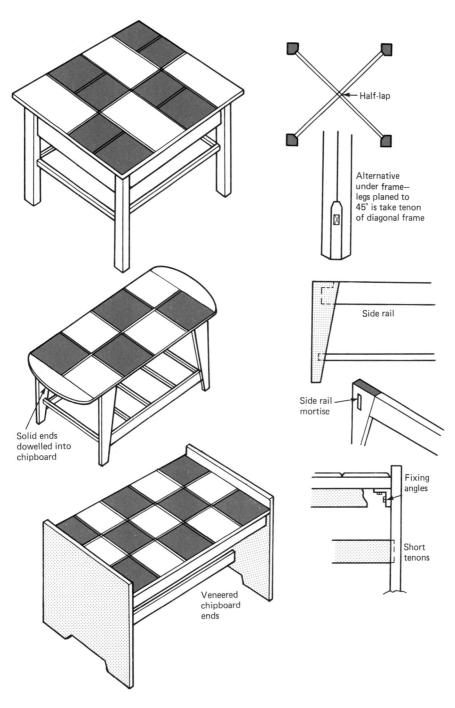

← Half-lap

Alternative
under frame—
legs planed to
45° is take tenon
of diagonal frame

Side rail

Side rail
mortise

Solid ends
dowelled into
chipboard

Fixing
angles

Short
tenons

Veneered
chipboard
ends

Square and rectangular tile-top tables

Top outline

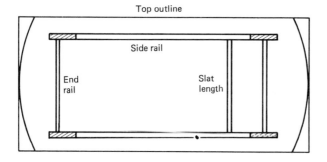

Side rail

End rail

Slat length

Plan gives length, width, shape of top, rail shoulder sizes, slat lengths and material thicknesses

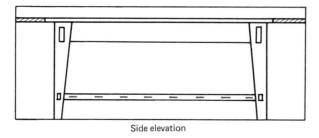

Side elevation gives height, leg shapes, size and position of end rail mortises, slat size and position

Side elevation

Setting-out for the tile-top table

Plane all pieces to size and mark out the joints from the rod. Cut the mortises and tenons and any shapes or moulds. Fit the assembly dry, cramp up and correct where necessary. Sand all edges smooth, then glue and assemble. Re-sand the surfaces and apply the finish as required.

Assemble the tiles to plan and bed them down to the (still loose) top panel. Use only the minimum amount of tile cement. Clean up with a damp cloth. Mitre the edgings and glue and pin them in place. Punch in the pins and fill the holes with wood filler. Wipe clean with a damp cloth. Apply a finish to match the underframe, then fit the top to the underframe using angle brackets.

Garden table with seats

This is planned as a softwood project entailing only accurate sawing, chamfering, drilling, screwing and, of course, sanding and finishing. The materials should be clean (knot-free), clear redwood (pine); although it should be knot-free, small golden knots may be tolerated. The assembly screws should be of brass, or brassed, to prevent rust. Other plated screws would do, but brass looks better. Also, if plated screw heads are damaged, rust will occur.

Decide on the size, although for obvious reasons this is partly predetermined; tables must be approximately 760 mm (30 in) high and seats 405–455 mm (16 –18 in) high. The width of the top may be increased or decreased, as may the width of the slatted seats and the overall length.

The slatted design is to allow water to drain away. Use urea adhesive throughout and finish with several coats of exterior polyurethane varnish (two-pack if possible), rubbing down smooth between each coating and applying only in warm, dry conditions.

Having decided on the size, make an end view drawing. If no paper or board is available that is large enough, use chalk on a garage floor; all you want is the angle of splay of the legs and their length. Only half of the end view need be drawn,

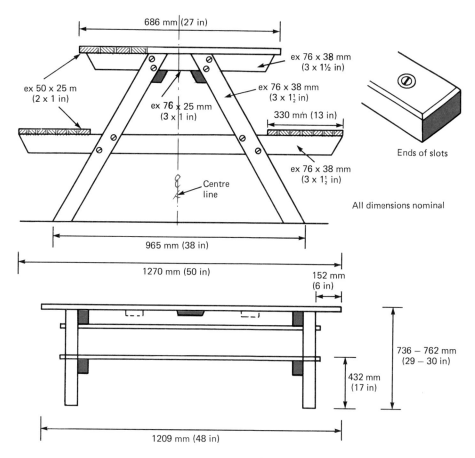

686 mm (27 in)

ex 76 x 38 mm (3 x 1½ in)

ex 50 x 25 m (2 x 1 in)

ex 76 x 38 mm (3 x 1½ in)

ex 76 x 25 mm (3 x 1 in)

330 mm (13 in)

Centre line

ex 76 x 38 mm (3 x 1½ in)

Ends of slots

All dimensions nominal

965 mm (38 in)

1270 mm (50 in)

152 mm (6 in)

736 – 762 mm (29 – 30 in)

432 mm (17 in)

1209 mm (48 in)

Slatted garden table with built-in seats

working from a centre line; the other side will be a mirror image.

Make a cutting list using a nominal 75 × 38 mm (3 × 1½ in) timber for the legs and framing and a nominal 50 × 25 mm (2 × 1 in) timber for the slats. Plan the slat spacing at about 12 mm (½ in), just wide enough to get the varnish brush in. The top stiffening slat could be a nominal 75 × 25 mm (3 × 1 in). Keep the seat length less than the top length to reduce possible centre sag.

Cut all pieces to a rough length. Mark out the angles of the legs and the angles on the ends of the cross rails; cut these accurately. Plane bevels on the top edges of the slats. Drill and countersink screw holes for the end frames and glue and fit

the end frames using 62 mm (2½ in) long No 10 countersunk screws. Lightly tack two battens across the seat supports to enable the end frames to stand up. Check on the overall length and adjust the battens until the job 'looks' right. Glue and fit on the two length stretchers below the top cross rails using 38 mm (1½ in) long No 8 screws. The edges of the stretchers should be bevelled to fit.

Drop on the top slats and mark the screw holes on one of them. Treat the seat in the same way. Then drill the holes in one top slat and in one seat slat. These two are then used as drilling guides for the rest of the slats. Countersink all holes and use 38 mm (1½ in) No 8 countersunk screws to fix all slats, using plywood spacers to maintain gaps. Apply a dab of adhesive below each slat. Make an entry

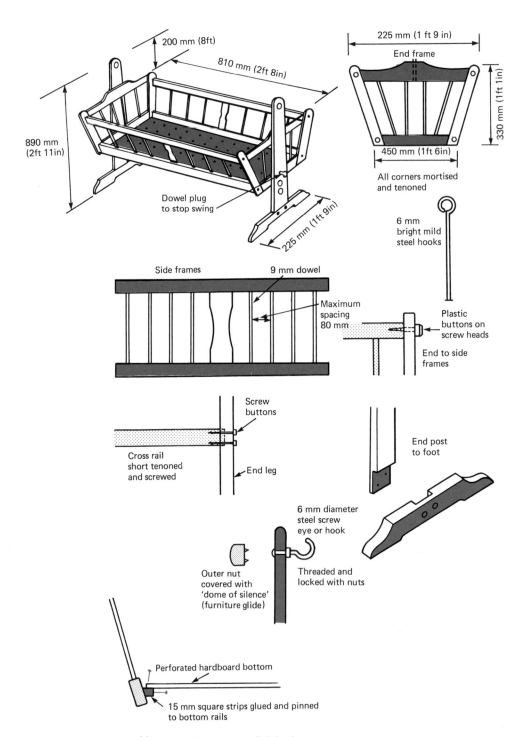

200 mm (8ft)

810 mm (2ft 8in)

890 mm
(2ft 11in)

Dowel plug
to stop swing

225 mm (1ft 9in)

225 mm (1 ft 9 in)

End frame

330 mm (1ft 1in)

450 mm (1ft 6in)

All corners mortised
and tenoned

6 mm
bright mild
steel hooks

Side frames

9 mm dowel

Maximum
spacing
80 mm

Plastic
buttons on
screw heads

End to side
frames

Screw
buttons

Cross rail
short tenoned
and screwed

End leg

End post
to foot

6 mm diameter
steel screw
eye or hook

Outer nut
covered with
'dome of silence'
(furniture glide)

Threaded and
locked with nuts

Perforated hardboard bottom

15 mm square strips glued and pinned
to bottom rails

Swinging crib of red beech, white-enamelled or clear-finished hole for all screws using a large bradawl. Trim the ends of the slats so that they are in a straight line. Use a Surform, or plane and rasp, to chamfer each slat end to match the side chamfer.

Turn the table over and fix the centre stiffener up into the top slats using 32 mm (1¼ in) No 8 screws. Two top cross stiffeners could be used instead of one, if thought necessary.

Sand all timber surfaces, smooth and apply the surface coating. Alternatives to a varnish finish are a coloured wood preservative or linseed oil brushed on and rubbed in. Both of these need a long time to dry and repeated applications each year.

Swinging crib

This is suitable for young babies, although some grow really active more quickly than others. As soon as the baby begins to sit up, the crib will tend to swing rather than to rock. At this stage consider transferring the baby to a standard cot. The crib can then be used as a doll's cot later on.

The materials needed are: red beech or ramin planed to 18 mm (¾ in) or slightly less; 9 mm (⅜ in) dowel; round steel 6 mm (¼ in) in diameter; two steel threaded eyes 25 mm (1 in) in diameter; a perforated peg board; 16 white plastic screw covers; two 'domes of silence'; screws and adhesive; sealer, white enamel or clear varnish; and oddments to make the bottom support battens and the plug to lock the swing.

Where shaped work is involved there must be a drawing. For this project the entire end elevation should be drawn. This will given the patterns on the crib top end rails, the angles for the tenon shoulders on the top and bottom rails, the height of the legs and the position of the leg mortise. The marking for the half-lap of the feet will be shown as well as the shape of the feet.

Remember that if the crib is to swing freely, its lower corners must be clear of the centre stretcher.

A simple plan on the centre line will give the shoulder length of the cross rail and the lengths of the crib side rails. It will also help if the dowel centres are worked out on the rod.

The materials

As all of the timber, apart from the shaped side slats at 9 mm (⅜ in) thick, is finished at approximately 18 mm (¾ in), the cutting list should be combined to enable you to buy only wide, planed boards of the required lengths and widths. Rip-sawing could be done at home. For example, the crib length is shorter than the height of the two end posts, so the minimum length of board would be the length required to cut these end posts. These finish at about 66 mm (2⅝ in) at the bottom, but taper towards the top. The stretcher rail, of about the same width, could be combined with these, so you would need a 915 × 225 mm (3 ft × 9 in) board.

The feet are the same width as the lower ends of the posts, as are the crib top end rails. Thus you will get both feet, both end top rails and two side rails from a 1070 × 225 mm (3½ ft × 9 in) board. The two remaining side rails, the four end uprights and the two crib bottom rails can be squeezed out of a 915 × 225 mm (3 ft × 9 in) board.

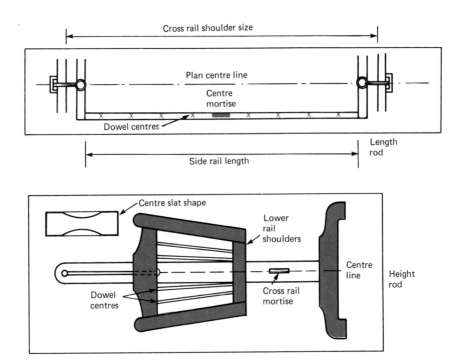

Setting-out for the crib

Bear in mind that all sizes for this sort of work can only be nominal. Design the job to suit the material.

The work

Mark out and rip-saw the straight rails and plane their edges to width. Mark out the four shaped pieces (the two feet and the two crib top end rails) and the two tapered end uprights. Leave any straight cuts and use either an electric profile saw or a hand bow or coping saw to cut out the shapes. Bear in mind it is easier to hold the board for cutting shapes if it is left as large as possible.

When all the shapes are cut, finish by planing the edges. Mark out 10 mortises (eight for the crib corners and two for the leg stretcher rail) and the eight angled tenons and two square tenons. Mark out

the bottom end post half-laps and the housings for these on the cross feet. Mark out and bore for the dowels and, if there are shaped slats, mark out four mortises for these. Remember to bore at an angle for the end dowels.

Cut all the mortises and tenons. Fit the end frames together and, while assembled, measure the dowel lengths. Fit the stretcher rail joints and the feet half-laps. Pre-bore for the screws on the crib corner posts, end posts and feet. Finally decorate with stopped chamfers, if desired. In any case, all edges and corners must be rounded. Sand down the work thoroughly. Glue and assemble the two side frames and two end frames. Assemble the leg posts on to the feet and glue and screw them in position. If the crib is likely to be dismantled later for storage, do not use adhesive on any joints other than the side dowels, end tenons and lower leg half-laps. Glue and pin the bottom supporting strips to the insides of the two end and two side frames.

Cramp the crib assembly and adjust the positions of the four corners. When all four corners match together, drill through the end frames into the ends of the four side rails; penetrate just far enough to mark these side rails. Change to a smaller drill size that will give a start to the screws and drill these holes. Slip the plastic screw buttons on the 50 mm (2 in) No 8 screws, grease the screws and tighten all eight of them. Fit the bottom hardboard. The crib is now complete apart from fitting the steel hangers and finishing the surface. Assemble the two end post frames together with the cross stretcher rail. Drill holes for the 50 mm (2 in) No 8 screws and tighten these four in place.

Rest the crib on the stretcher and finalise the sizes of the upright metal hooks and the projecting screw eye that will go together to make the pivots. The points to look for here are end clearance, stretcher rail clearance and firm fixing of the eyes into the end post.

Having made up these pieces of metal work, drill two holes for the rods down through the crib end rails. The lower ends of these two swinging rods may be rivetted over, with a washer between the rivetted end and the wood, or they may be threaded. A larger hole will be needed in the rail lower edge for the nut and the washer to fit into. Finishing will be more straight forward if the screwed joints are dismantled.

Picture framing

Without a complementary frame no picture will appear at its best. Each picture must be mounted and framed individually, with the mount, if needed, and the frame made up by craftwork.

Simple mitred framing has been described in Chapter 5. But although many people with a picture to frame consult a friendly woodworker, skilled as he may be, he may not necessarily have the basic knowledge of framing that is required for a good presentation.

The artwork

Oil colour paintings on canvas are not glazed; nor are they normally mounted. In general they are put directly into the rebate on the frame and are left on the stretcher frame of the canvas. Oil paintings on other materials are also directly framed.

Coloured prints, line drawings and photographs are always glazed, with an air gap between the face of the artwork and the inner face of the glass. This gap is provided by the mount. Colour photographs may be displayed full out to the frame without a border mount and without an air gap. The balance between colour, composition and size will give you a basis for deciding on treatment.

The mount

The mount is of pastel-coloured card, sold as mount card in art shops. The card colour must compliment the picture, so take the picture when choosing the mount. Experiment to determine the relative size of the mount to the picture, for a small, brilliant picture may be suited to either a broad, neutral (light grey) mount on to a narrower, darker mount.

Mark out the window in the mount (through which the picture will show) and cut it out with a very sharp craft knife. If

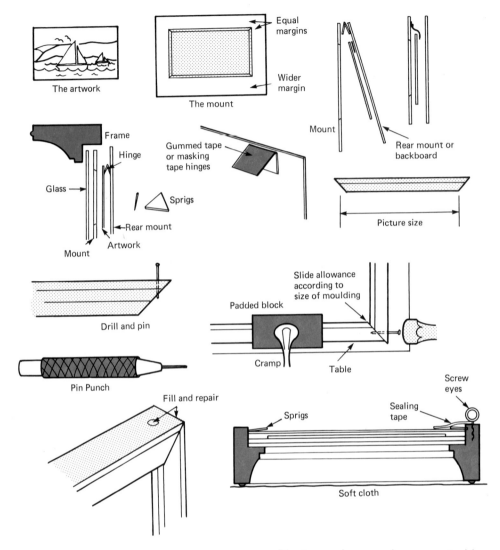

Picture-framing details

possible, angle the knife edge to produce an angled cut. Fine abrasive paper will remove any whiskers left. Cut down on to a sheet of glass or on to the smooth face of hardboard.

The artwork may be taped (from top edge only, to allow for slight stretching) to the back of the mount card, or it may be taped to a rear mount card with the two cards being taped together to form a sandwich with the artwork. There must be no fixing other than at the top; the picture is always hung.

Photographs may be mounted by using a spray-on photo-mount adhesive on their backs and then smoothing them down on to an oversized piece of mount card. The border is then trimmed and the photograph goes directly to the glass.

The frame

Check frame samples against the mounted artwork (although you could choose the frame when you buy the mount card) and determine the style and colour required. Some of the gold and black framing available goes well with bright-coloured prints and photographs, for example.

Measure the mount card, mark the rebates and cut the mitres. Leave any slight whiskers, for these combine with the adhesive to lock the corners together. Try the frame dry, both for accurate mitres and for rebate size. If the mitres are very slightly out, correct them using a very sharp bevel edge chisel, taking a shearing cut lightly across high spots. However carefully you work, there will always be slight chipping of the gold and black enamels.

Pre-drill the top and bottom frame members to take fine panel pins. Glue and pin the frame parts to produce two 'L' pieces. Check for fit and glue the two 'L' pieces together. Pin the last two corners and check for squareness.

Clean off any surplus adhesive and fill the holes left as you punched in the pins with either a black filler for a black frame or a neutral filler for a coloured frame. When the filler is dry, sand it very lightly and touch it up with water paint from a child's paint box until the colour matches. Treat chipped corners in the same way. Finally touch in the painted spots with shellac lacquer (French polish). The gold (if any) will need touching in with a suitably matched gold colour or fluid gold wax.

Assembly

Take the frame to a glass shop and have a 2 mm piece of glass the correct size put in. Clean the glass with a proprietary window cleaner and wash it over with methylated spirit. Dry and polish it and lay it in the frame, which must face down on a protecting cloth. Re-polish the inner glass face and drop in the mounted artwork. Press this firmly down and raise the picture to inspect the front. Hold it to a bright light to catch any finger marks, dust or cat's hairs, for example, trapped inside.

Then put in the back board if needed (the mount card may be sufficient on small pictures) and press it down with one hand while pushing several small pins into the outer wall of the rebate to hold it there. Special sprigs may be bought for this, but short panel pins will hold in the picture assembly. Pin at 50 mm (2 in) intervals, driving in the pins with a light hammer. Slide the hammer along the rear card and support the frame edge against a cloth-wrapped piece of heavy timber. This prevents 'bounce' while you hammer. Use masking tape to seal the rebate completely against dust. Touch in any missed spots on the corners and polish up the glass again.

Hanging

Make holes with a bradawl for the screw eyes at a third of the way down each side of the frame at the back. Fix in the screw eyes. Use either nylon hanging cord or fine woven brass wire to form the hanging loop, carefully double-knotting the cord or twisting the trailing ends of wire for a neat finish.

Embroidery frame

This frame should be made as light as possible. To give sufficient strength in small sections, the framing should be of steamed becch (red beech) and the pivots

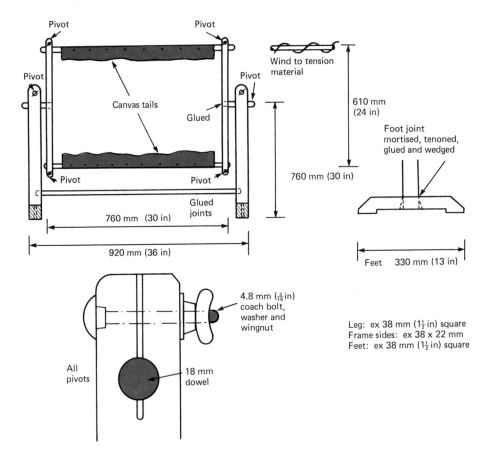

Pivot   Pivot

Pivot   Canvas tails   Pivot   Wind to tension material

Glued

Pivot   Pivot

Glued joints

760 mm (30 in)

920 mm (36 in)

610 mm (24 in)

Foot joint mortised, tenoned, glued and wedged

760 mm (30 in)

Feet   330 mm (13 in)

4.8 mm ($\frac{3}{16}$ in) coach bolt, washer and wingnut

All pivots

18 mm dowel

Leg: ex 38 mm (1$\frac{1}{2}$ in) square
Frame sides: ex 38 x 22 mm
Feet: ex 38 mm (1$\frac{1}{2}$ in) square

Embroidery frame

and rollers of 18 mm (¾ in) diameter hardwood dowels. The bottom cross stretcher should also be of 18 mm (¾ in) dowel.

The principle of the design is that all six pivots are formed by boring 18 mm (¾ in) holes and then cutting down slots with a handsaw. The wing nuts should never be screwed tight if there are no dowels in the holes. The embroidery material is tack-stitched to the top and bottom roller canvasses and the rollers are then twisted to achieve the correct tension. The side pivots are short pieces of dowel glued into the side frame members.

All corners of the wood sections should be rounded to a noticeable degree and all surfaces finely sanded. The top finish will be clear lacquer. If found necessary, canvas tails could be tacked to the side frame members.

Further helpful reading

Beginner's Guides are pocket-sized but contain an enormous amount of information of interest to DIY enthusiasts, from novices to old hands who insist they are well past the 'beginner' stage!

For example, **Beginner's Guide to Domestic Plumbing** gives clear, concise coverage, with detailed illustrations, of all that the householder needs to know about domestic plumbing design and materials, the techniques of hot and cold water supply, sanitary installations and drainage. For those easily baffled by electrics, **Beginner's Guide to Electric Wiring** is an easily readable yet authoritative guide requiring no previous technical knowledge. It covers the planning and installation of wiring, accessories and fittings in the home and workshop — always with the emphasis on safety and conformity with the Wiring Regulations. If you want to produce well-finished woodwork, **Beginner's Guide to Woodworking** is an introduction to this satisfying craft that will increase both theoretical knowledge and practical skill. It describes clearly the tools and methods used by professional carpenters and joiners, so that the reader can put into practice their basic techniques.

For the more ambitious do-it-yourselfer, **Beginner's Guide to Building Construction** introduces the principles of construction, providing the knowledge that is essential for making a success of any building job, whether a small home extension or a complete structure, from the foundation to the roof and drains.

Fuel and power costs are an increasing worry for every householder. **Beginner's Guide to Home Energy Saving** gives down-to-earth guidance on minimising the bills. Possibilities described range from no-cost 'energy housekeeping' measures to investments, large and small, in insulation and other improvements — not forgetting possible snags and side-effects. **Beginner's Guide to Central Heating** provides an understanding of central heating in its many forms, so that both intending owners and existing owners whose heating equipment needs replacing can choose the most effective and economical system. The author also gives advice on efficient heating control.

These are all available from bookshops. The series also includes guides to various craft and hobby subjects such as radio and electronics, photography and computers. New titles are added continually, and a colour brochure is available from:

Newnes Technical Books
Borough Green, Sevenoaks, Kent TN15 8PH

QUESTIONS & ANSWERS
books to extend your skills...

These compact **Questions & Answers** books are a great source of help to the do-it-yourselfer up against an unfamiliar problem. Some typical questions dealt with in eight of the books are shown below – and there are lots of other titles, from **Radio Repair** to **GRP Boat Construction**.

Painting and Decorating   How can stains on walls and ceilings be prevented? What is the correct way to paint a panelled door? How is rust removed and treated? What causes paint to crack or flake? How is wallpaper hung in an angle? How is mould growth treated?

Brickwork and Blockwork   What are the basic types of brick? What is meant by bonding? How is a cavity wall built? How are door and window frames fixed into openings? How are arches supported during construction? How is stone cladding fixed to the face of a building?

Carpentry and Joinery   What are the basic measuring and marking-out tools? What are the basic framing joints? How are doors fitted and hung? How are openings formed in timber floors? How are preservatives applied to timbers? How is a close-boarded fence constructed?

Plastering   When is lime used in plastering? How is a floating coat applied? How are square external angles formed? What is a cold-pour skin mould? How are curved mouldings run? How are fibrous plaster casts made? What causes plaster to set too slowly?

Electric Wiring   How do you choose a wiring system? What precautions should you take when laying cables? What is a single-pole switch? Why are most electric lamps connected in parallel? What is a ring final sub-circuit? How do you test an electrical installation?

Domestic Lighting   What is 'good lighting'? How can a room be lighted without excessive glare? How do fluorescent lamps work? How do emergency lighting systems work? How does an earth-leakage circuit-breaker work? How do you light a front garden or drive?

Plumbing   What is a one-pipe system? What is a rising main? How are pipes jointed? How can water hammer be prevented? How does a flushing cistern work? What materials are used for drainage pipes? How are drains and sanitary systems tested?

Central Heating   What central heating systems are available? What are the advantages of a wet system? What is the choice among gas boilers? How should I design a full ducted system? Which fuel should I choose? What are the essential controls?

These are all available from bookshops. For further information please write to:

ewnes Technical Books
Borough Green, Sevenoaks, Kent TN15 8PH

Index

Abrasives, 51–52
Acid catalyst lacquers, 73, 74
Adhesives, 56–58
   casein, 57
   cleaning surplus, 58–59, 71
   cramping times, 58
   mixing, 57
   PVA, 57
   urea, 57, 58
Assembly, 52–56

Batten board, 18, 19
Beech, 16, 90
Bench, 3
Bench hook, 9, 10
Bevel chisels, 7
Blockboard, 18, 19
Box dovetail, 45

Carcase joints, 44–45
Casein-based adhesives, 57
Cellulose finish, 74
Chipboard, 18–19
   corner battens, 40
   dowelling, 39–40
   knock-down fittings, 27–29, 79, 84–86
Chisels, 7
   bevelled, 7
   firmer, 7
   mortise, 7–8
   paring, 8
Choosing wood, 17
Cleaning away surplus adhesive, 58–59, 71
Coloured lacquer, 74
Complex marking, 70
Cramp pads, 71
Cramping methods, 52–55
   alternative methods, 55–56
   squaring up, 55, 56
Creosote, 72
Cross halving, 43
Custom board, 19, 21
Cutting lists, 64, 67

Deal, 13
Door catches, 28, 29
Douglas fir, 13

Dovetailed joints, 38–39, 44, 45, 46
   box, 45
   cutting, 38, 39, 45–46
   secret lap, 45
   secret mitre, 44, 45
   template, 38, 45–46
Dowelling, 36–37
   chipboard, 39–40
Drawings, 60–70
Drill, electric, 11

Edge-to-edge joints, 36
Edging strips for chipboard, 29
Electric tools,
   drill, 11
   jigsaw, 11, 12
   purpose-made units, 12
   sander, 11
   saw, 11
Embroidery frame, 95–96
Enamel, 73

Filling, 72–73, 75
Finishes,
   acid catalyst, 73, 74
   cellulose, 74
   creosote, 72
   enamel, 73
   french polish, 75–76
   lacquers, 73
   linseed oil, 77
   paint, 72, 73
   polyurethane, 74
   priming, 72
   teak oil, 17, 77
   top coat, 73
Finishing, 71–78
Firmer chisel, 7
Fittings and fixing, 22–29
   for chipboard, 27–29
Framing joints, 30, 31
French polish, 75–76

Garden table, 88, 89
Golden walnut, 17

Hammers, 9
Hand tools, 3–10
Hardboard conditioning, 73
Hardwoods, 15–17
   beech, 16, 90
   golden walnut, 17
   mahogany, 16
   meranti, 16–17

Hardwoods *continued*
  oak, 15
  ramin, 16, 90
  sapele, 16
  teak, 17
  utile, 16
Hemlock, 13, 14
Hi-fi unit, 79–86
  cleaning, 86
  cutting panels, 83
  fittings, 80, 84
  materials, 79, 80
  setting out, 81
Hollow walls, fixing to, 22–23
Housings, 32–33, 45
  lapped, 46–47
  tongued, 46

Iron-on-edging, 84

Jigsaw, 11, 12
Joint types,
  carcase, 44–45
  cross-halvings, 43
  dovetailed, 38–39, 44, 45–46
  dowelled, 36–37, 39–40
  edge-to-edge, 36
  framing, 30, 31
  half-laps, 31–32
  housings, 32–33, 45, 46–47
  laps, 47–48
  mitres, 38, 41–43
  mortise and tenons, 33–35, 43–44
  multiple tenons, 47
  nailed, 30
  scarfed, 47–48
  variations, 48–50

'Knock-down' fittings, 27–28, 79, 84–86
Knotting, 72

Lacquer finishes, 73
  coloured, 74
Linseed oil, 77

Man-made boards, 18–20
  batten board, 18, 19
  blockboard, 18, 19
  chipboard, 18, 19, 20
  custom board, 19, 21
  plywood, 18
Marking out, 60, 69–70
  complex parts, 70
  tools, 7

Material sizes, 35
Materials,
  hardwoods, 15–17
  man-made boards, 18–20
  softwoods, 13–14
Measuring, 60–61
  tools, 60
Mitre box, 9, 10, 41, 42
Mitre cutting, 41, 42
  template, 48
Mitred mouldings, 48, 50
Mitres, 38
Mortise chisels, 7
Mortise cutting, 8
Moulded rails, 34–35, 48, 50
Multiple tenons, 47

Nailed joints, 30
Nails, 23, 24

Oak, 15
Orbital sander, 11
Order of work (painting), 73

Paint, 72, 73
Painting hardboard, 73
Pairs, 70
Parana pine, 14, 36
Paring chisel, 8
Picture framing, 41, 42, 93–95
  assembly, 94–95
  mounts, 93
  planning, 93
Pinch rods, 60, 61
Planes, 5–7
Planing, 5–6
Plumb bob, 60, 61
Plywood, 18
Polishing, french, 75, 76
  bodying, 76
  spiriting, 76
  shortcuts, 75
  surface filling, 75
Polyurethane finish, 74
Polyvinyl acetate (PVA), 57
Power tools, 11, 12
Pozidriv screws, 24, 25
Primer, 72
Projects, 79–96
  embroidery frame, 95, 96
  garden table, 88–89
  hi-fi unit, 79–86
  picture framing (see also 41–42), 93–95
  swinging crib, 91–93
  tiled table, 86–88